W9-DGS-634

Grieg

Robert Layton

Other titles in the series

The Illustrated Lives of the Great Composers.

Grieg

Robert Layton

OMNIBUS PRESS

London/New York/Sydney

For my friend Simon Emes,
this little introduction to a world he knows so well.

Cover design and art direction by Pearce Marchbank
Cover photography by Julian Hawkins
Text design, scanning and film origination by Hilite

Copyright © 1998 by Robert Layton
This edition published in 1998 by Omnibus Press, a division of Book Sales Limited

ISBN 0.7119.4811.9
Order No. OP47745

Exclusive Distributors
Book Sales Limited,
8/9 Frith Street,
London W1V 5TZ, UK.

Music Sales Corporation,
257 Park Avenue South,
New York, NY 10010, USA

Five Mile Press,
22 Summit Road, Noble Park,
Victoria 3174, Australia.

To the Music Trade only
Music Sales Limited,
8/9 Frith Street,
London W1V 5TZ, UK.

Photo credits:

Mary Evans Picture Library: 13,14,22,41,42,44,59,84;
Fotomas Index: 11; Peter Joslin: 73,108,119,135,137,140,146;
Lebrecht Collection: 7,16,20,23,25,26,27,30,31,33,36,48,50,53,54,55,57,58,60,
64,65,71,75,80,81,86,88,95,97,99,102,104,105,106,107,109,110,111,112,114,115,
116,117,118,121,123,127,129,131,138,142,144,145,147,149,150,151,152,153;
Mansell Collection: 17,24,28,56,78,100; Rex Features: 8,9,15.

Printed in the United Kingdom by Redwood Books, Trowbridge, Wiltshire.

A catalogue record for this book is available from the British Library.

Visit Omnibus Press at http://www.omnibuspress.com

Contents

Foreword

An American writer, reviewing Eleanor Bailie's *Grieg: The Pianist's Repertoire* in 1996, spoke of the English-language literature on Grieg as "sparse". As a glance at the checklist of books at the back of this volume will show, nothing can be further from the truth. Indeed, when I was at first asked to write this short life of the composer, I demurred. Apart from Ms Bailie's excellent volume, recent years have brought us a study of the songs by Beryl Foster, and above all, the definitive *Edvard Grieg, The Man and the Artist* by Finn Benestad and Dag Schjelderup-Ebbe, sumptuously illustrated with colour plates and photos as well as copious musical examples. This volume examines the music with authority and reveals Grieg's life story in greater detail than any previous study has - and any future biographer could! Moreover, while John Horton's *Grieg* volume in the *Master Musicians* series remains in print, there seems little need for yet another book in English.

However, Grieg is a much-loved composer and it would be a pity if he were unrepresented in this series. Of course, this account of his life is greatly indebted, as will be others for many years to come, to Professor Benestad and Professor Schjelderup-Ebbe's scholarship. To them go grateful thanks, as well as to Dr Lionel Carley whose Grieg and Delius and his many learned papers have broadened our picture of the composer. My thanks are also due to Torbjørn Støverud of the Grieg Society, for his kindness in reading through this volume and for his helpful comments, and of course, to my copy editor, Constance Novis.

R.L.

Edvard Grieg.
Painted by
Erik Werenskiold
in 1891-92.

Chapter 1

Norway's voice in the world

Edvard Grieg is one of the handful of popular composers through whom many find their way to music. There is something perennially fresh and immediate about him: his musical language resonates because it is firmly rooted in place in much the same way as are Janáček, Copland, Falla or Vaughan Williams. After all, you have only to hear a bar of their music or that of Grieg's friend Delius, to know exactly where you are in the world. What is it about their musical language that so clearly conveys their national identity? For surely there is no doubt about the Englishness of Delius, whose music immediately transports us to the luxuriant summer gardens of England just as Copland breathes the wide open spaces of the Prairies. In much the same way a few bars of Grieg bring the listener to a completely distinctive terrain. Indeed, one can speak of him as Norway's voice in the world.

Grieg's music is so familiar that we tend to take it for granted, and as a result Grieg has been as underrated in recent years as he was overexposed in the past. The popularity of

Norway's coastline

which he himself complained did for a time have the adverse effect he feared. The few hackneyed pieces somehow hindered the acceptance of his more substantial music. But in a sense his popularity was illusory for the wider musical public never really found its way much further than *Peer Gynt*, the *Lyric Suite* and the Piano Concerto and a handful of popular piano pieces and songs. Such masterpieces as *Haugtussa* (*The Mountain Maid*), op.67 and the *Norwegian Peasant Dances* (*Slåtter*), op. 72 were always rarities. But Grieg's sense of harmonic colour and fresh melodic invention won him a huge following during his lifetime and well beyond.

Western Norway

Norway possesses the longest and most spectacular coastline in Europe. From its northernmost point in the Arctic circle to its southern extremity it encompasses over 2,650 kilometres or 1,700 miles, though if its fjords and inlets are included its coastland extends to no fewer than 21,465 kilometres. Its longest fjord is over 204 kilometres, its largest glacier 487 kilometres and its longest river 600 kilometres! The grandeur and magnificence of its fjords and the waterfalls, the largest being 300 metres, make an indelible impression on visitors.

As early as AD 800, Vikings set sail from these fjords, carrying out raids on European coastal settlements. Vikings, or Norsemen, came from Sweden and Denmark, as well as Norway. During the Viking era (ninth to the eleventh centuries), Norway's population was little more than 100,000, yet Viking ships set sail on their missions of trade and plunder, from the Baltic and the Black Sea, to England and Ireland. Norwegian Vikings raided Scotland, Ireland and France and colonized the Hebrides, Orkneys, the Færoes, Iceland and

Greenland. Norwegian Vikings were also among the very first Europeans to reach North America – Viking remains have been found at Newfoundland, in Canada. Skilled shipbuilders and expert navigators, Vikings were able to undertake long sea voyages and were the terror of Europe. Despite their ferocious reputation, Vikings also traded and established permanent settlements and had a profound influence on the course of European history.

Norway's present prosperity is a recent phenomenon, largely a product of North Sea oil and the prudent management of its resources. Indeed it is one of the most prosperous countries in the world today, and very different from the country which Grieg and his contemporaries would have known. If prosperity was late in coming, so early in its history was Christianity. Norway was not brought into the Christian fold until 995, when King Olav's conversion opened the doors to priests and monks from the wider European world. In the early Middle Ages, Norway possessed a strong civil government whose writ ran as far as Iceland, Greenland, and in the east the Swedish province of Jämtland. Its empire even included the Isle of Man, the small island between England and Ireland. Indeed up until 1350 it was both an independent and relatively flourishing country. However the Black Death affected it more severely than most European countries; and far from decimating its population actually halved it. It dropped from 450,00 at the beginning of the fourteenth century to less than 200,000 and so severe were the ravages of the plague that whole communities were wiped out, and farmsteads lay deserted. By 1536 government had virtually collapsed and Norway finally came under the Danish crown. As King Christian III's accession charter put it, "Because the political power and wealth of the realm of Norway have disintegrated and Norway's citizens are no longer capable of supporting a lord and king ... the realm shall hereafter be and remain under the Danish crown in the same manner as the other lands, Jutland, Fyn and Skåne (Southern Sweden) and hereafter neither be nor be called a separate kingdom but a part of the realm of Denmark and under the Danish crown for time everlasting." At first Norway was governed by a national council which ruled in concert with the monarch but in 1660, the year in which Charles II returned to England, King Frederick III introduced absolute rule.

"Time everlasting" turned out to be the next three centuries. In 1814, the end of the Napoleonic era, Norway gained its independence from Denmark. During the intervening years it had prospered materially. Its population at the time of the union had fallen to 150,000 but by 1800, thanks to lower infant mortality, had risen to 880,000. Agriculture, fishing and forestry had grown during the union – and above all, so had shipping. Norway had become one of the leading seafaring countries in Europe, and timber and fish were among its chief exports.

The Napoleonic upheaval left no part of Europe untouched. In 1807 Denmark–Norway was drawn into the conflict when

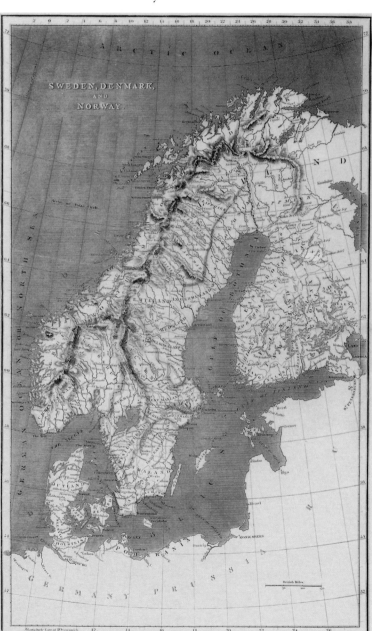

Map of the Scandinavian countries and Finland.

England imposed a blockade on trade with France. Admiral Nelson's fleet had eventually bombarbed Copenhagen to enforce the restriction. As the war entered its concluding phase, the great powers re-drew the map of Europe. Denmark had not supported the winning side and was owed no favours. On the other hand, Norway's newfound independence was far from unconditional. Under the Treaty of Kiel in 1814, it had been ceded by the Allied coalition to Sweden. The days when Sweden had been a great power had long passed, and in 1809 Sweden in turn had been forced to cede Finland to Russia. Sweden had governed Finland for nearly six centuries and Norway was a kind of consolation prize. The resultant stand-off between the Norwegians and their powerful Swedish neighbour occupied the best part of the year and there was even a brief period of hostilities lasting a couple of weeks before a solution emerged. The eventual outcome was the formula of two countries, one sovereign. To all intents and purposes, the Norwegians were left to order their own affairs and had their own constitution and parliament, the *Storting*. However, foreign affairs, consular representation abroad and defence were not separate but decided jointly in Stockholm, and the Swedish King became the Norwegian Head of State.

All the national sentiment long directed against Danish rule was gradually to be mobilised against Sweden and slowly gathered force during the remainder of the century. All the same Norway had enjoyed increasing prosperity during the union with Denmark, and the emergence of a better-educated middle class had sown the seeds of a more vital cultural life. Musical life was relatively undeveloped, and there was nowhere comparable with the fare that Copenhagen or Stockholm could offer. Norway was still a largely peasant community, a rural small-holding backwater. Yet Bergen, Norway's window on the outside world and its most important trading city, could boast the *Harmonien*, the direct forerunner of the Bergen Philharmonic. This is the earliest permanent orchestra in continuous existence in Europe, and older even than the Leipzig Gewandhaus, though not, of course, comparable in quality. Many of its musicians were from the European mainland and few native Norwegians made much more than a local reputation. Further north in Trondheim, Norway's first capital city where Olav had planted the seeds of Christianity in the tenth century, there was also some musical activity. For example, the composer Johan Daniel Berlin, who came from Memel settled there in the 1760s. But nothing emerged that you could remotely call Norwegian. While the Swedish Court could foster an active musical life, both before and at the time of Gustav III, encouraging such composers as Johan Helmich Roman, Naumann and Joseph Martin Kraus, there was no Norwegian court to do the same – and to be fair, little indigenous creative talent to sustain. For the remainder of the nineteenth century Norway could be said to be searching for a national identity. Grieg's music and the plays of Henrik Ibsen and Bjørnstjerne Bjørnson, were part of this quest. Ibsen's plays still occupy a commanding position on the world stage but Bjørnson's have fallen out of the repertoire. Yet he was perhaps the dominant force in Grieg's Norway.

Bergen in the 1840s.

Chapter 2

Greig or Grieg

On his father's side the Grieg family can trace its forebears back several generations to Scotland. The name was then spelt Greig but pronounced Gregg. John Greig, the composer's great-great-grandfather came from Rathen, a village some 50 or so miles northeast of Aberdeen. His son, Alexander moved to Bergen in 1770, where at the end of that decade he adopted Norwegian citizenship and changed his name from Greig to Grieg. Alexander had strong Stuart sympathies and emigrated to Norway in the wake of the battle of Culloden, which brutally put paid to the Stuart cause. Norway's strong links with

Old Bergen as Grieg would have known it.

Scotland, both culturally and linguistically, would make Bergen an obvious choice. Alexander Grieg soon built up a flourishing business, exporting fish and lobster to Britain and by the end of the century had become, albeit briefly, the British vice-consul in his adopted town. The business prospered and was passed in its turn to his son, John, who showed signs of the musical talent that was to emerge so strongly in his grandson. John Grieg took an active part in the musical life of Bergen and played in the orchestra, the so-called *Harmonien*. John's wife, too, had musical connections. She was the daughter of Nils Haslund who was one of the first conductors of the *Harmonien* and also a violinist of note. John Grieg followed the family tradition and became British consul and in the fullness of time both the business and the consulship passed to his son, Alexander – Edvard Grieg's

Hanseatic buildings in Bergen.

father. The business still prospered and it was not long before he married, taking as his wife, Gesine Hagerup. Her father, also an Edvard, was a member of the *Storting* (Norwegian parliament), and represented Bergen between 1814–24. Later on, he became president of the upper house, the *Lagting*.

Gesine, Grieg's mother, was by all accounts a fine musician. Unusually, given the social constraints of the period, her parents allowed her to study both the piano and singing in Hamburg. On her return to Norway at the age of 19, she sang Agathe's aria from Weber's opera, *Der Freischütz* with the Bergen Orchestra. However, she abandoned singing for the piano, becoming in time a much sought-after teacher and a fine accompanist. Among the artists she accompanied was none other than the famous violinist Ole Bull, to whom she was also related, albeit distantly. It was Gesine who inherited Landås, the estate where the young Grieg would spend the summer months. Her father Edvard had willed his other house, Haukeland, to her brother Hermann. It was his daughter, Nina Hagerup, born in 1845, who was eventually to become the composer's wife.

Alexander Grieg was not Gesine's first choice as a husband. Her father, a civil servant, had refused her permission to marry the sailor with whom she had fallen in love. Love matches across the social boundaries were rare in the nineteenth century and marrying someone perceived to be of a lower class or "below her station", would have brought opprobium on the family. Alexander and Gesine married in 1836. She bore him

Grieg's home at Landås outside Bergen to which the family moved in 1853.

five children in all, of which Edvard, born a few days before midsummer, on 15 June 1843, was fourth.

The Grieg family lived in a house in Strandgaten in the old part of Bergen, not far from the famous Hanseatic buildings which still survive along the quay, so the young Edvard could watch the ships set sail for England, laden with his father's fish and fresh lobsters. Strandgaten was a bustling street which in the 1850s housed two bakers, a brewery, a smithy, which was

16

quite close to the Grieg household, an occulist, a tailor and a shoemaker. Not far away there were the offices of the Bergen Steamship Company and the names of other shipowners, like Schröder, Döscher, Silchenstedt and Prahl indicated that they, like the Grieg family, were of immigrant origin. The Grieg home, as befits a British vice-consul, consisted of two storeys with an attic, seven rooms in all, plus an outside building with a cellar and big stove as well as horse stalls and a wagon-shed.

Grieg's childhood, if his own account is to be believed, was happy and harmonious. He soon showed some signs of musical ability and enjoyed dreamily improvising at the piano. Gesine

Ole Bull who commanded Grieg's parents to send him to Leipzig.

took his musical education in hand and tried to instill some discipline into his studies without inhibiting his exploratory imagination. Shortly before his tenth birthday he was enrolled at a school of good standing in Bergen, *Tanks skole*, where he would have learned a wide variety of subjects: German, English and French, Religion, History, Geography, Maths and, of course, Norwegian. The school still survives and indeed flourishes in Bergen. These were the days before mandatory universal education, and most well-off families would either have sent their sons to private teachers, or have engaged a tutor to come to the home. Edvard did not particularly distinguish himself at school and went to some trouble to get out of it. Later in life in an article, *My First Success*, he recalled:

From the time that I was ten years old my parents lived during the summers at our lovely country home, Landås just a short distance from Bergen. Every single morning my elder brother and I had to trudge off to school in the pouring rain for which Bergen is famous. But I used this pouring rain in what I thought was a very clever boyish prank.

The rule at school was that a student who came late would not be admitted to the class, but as a punishment had to stand outside until the end of the period ... One rainy day when it happened – and it happened often – that I came to school entirely unprepared, I arranged so that I not only came a little late, but I stayed down on the street where I positioned myself under a drainpipe of a house until I became absolutely soaked to the skin. When I was finally admitted to the schoolroom, such rivulets of water streamed from my clothes down to the floor that the teacher – for the sake of both my classmates and me – couldn't defend detaining me, but immediately sent me home for a change of clothes. Because of the long distance to my home, this was the same as excusing me from morning school.

That I repeated this experiment rather often was already risky, but when I finally went so far as to come to school soaking wet one day when it was hardly raining, they became suspicious and sent someone out to spy on me. One fine day I got caught, and then I received a memorable introduction to the "percussion instruments".

Edvard was not a prodigy and did not at first entertain musical ambitions; moreover he was overshadowed at first by his older sister, Maren – who was to follow the example of her mother and became a well-known piano teacher – and his older brother, John whose instrument was the cello. But it soon became obvious that his gifts entitled him to a more advanced musical schooling than anything he was likely to receive in Bergen. A glance at the photos of him taken in his early adolescence reveals a sensitive nature and light, penetrating eyes. He was of a thoughtful yet at the same time vivacious temperament and already of the diminutive stature that was to distinguish him in maturity. His appearance was captured by one of his first biographers, Gerhard Schjelderup who was 16 years younger than the composer. He wrote of Grieg's delicate features:

"The fine serene forehead he had in common with many a creative artist. His light blue eyes under the bushy eyebrows sparkled like those of a child when listening to a fairy tale. They mostly had a joyful though gentle, dreamy expression, but when roused to sudden anger or indignation they could flash lightning. For with his short stumpy nose, the fine flowing hair, the firm expressive mouth under the strong moustache, and the resolute chin, he had dynamic energy and an impatient and passionate temperament. As in Wagner's features there was in his a marked contrast between the upper and lower parts of the face. The forehead reveals the dreamer, the mouth and chin a strong determination to live a life of untiring activity."

Edvard's general education did not progress altogether smoothly. In his third year he did not do well enough to proceed to the fourth but had to repeat the third all over again. Composition began to occupy him from the age of about nine and it soon became evident that music was to be his calling. He proudly took one of his compositions to school, "Variations on a German Melody for Piano by Edvard Grieg", only to be sneered at by his German teacher, "Next time you will bring your German dictionary to class, as you are supposed to, and leave such rubbish at home."

Stepping aside and looking at the wider musical scene for a moment, the young Grieg belongs to the same generation as Rimsky-Korsakov, Dvořák, Tchaikovsky and Fauré. If you think of them all being together at the same school, Grieg and Rimsky-Korsakov would have been classmates, Sullivan would have been in the class above them, while Tchaikovsky, Dvořák and Svendsen would have been three forms ahead. Bizet, Balakirev, Max Bruch and Mussorgsky would be preparing to leave school. During the early to mid-1840s, Schumann was composing *Dichterliebe* and his first two symphonies and piano concerto, Mendelssohn his *Scottish Symphony*, and nearer to home, the Danish composer Niels Gade was making a name for himself with his Overture, *Echoes of Ossian* and his first symphony.

By the summer of 1858 when he was fifteen, the Grieg family was wondering how best to proceed in furthering his musical education when the matter was decided for them. One day in August, their famous relative, the violinist and composer Ole Bull came to Landås. Gesine's sister, Johanne Margrethe had married Ole Bull's brother, Jens but Grieg's parents were less swayed by any blood ties than his sheer force of character and his fame.

Ole Bull would have been an outsize personality in any era. Most musical visitors to Bergen these days see Grieg's home, Troldhaugen and some make the pilgrimage to Bull's

A family picture from Landås taken in the 1850s. The young Edvard (seated and with hat) is fourth from the left. His father and mother are on the right and his brother John stands behind them with his back to the tree.

extraordinary Mauresque miniature palace, Lysøen. He built it towards the end of his life on a 650-acre island south of the city. No one visiting the house with its extraordinary mixture of styles could doubt that Bull was no ordinary man. Indeed he could be thought of as a precursor of the present-day jet-setter, for he played in the United States, Germany, France, England, Spain, Russia, Ireland, Egypt, Canada, Cuba and even Algeria. Inured as we are today to easy travel, these were days when it was arduous; his journey from Rome to Paris in 1836 by stage-coach took two weeks. Moreover he was far more than just

20

another itinerant virtuoso; he was a national figure and an ardent nationalist. He founded Norway's National Theatre, and was also to found an utopian colony for Norwegian immigrants in the United States. Yet his nationalism was not tinged by the anti-Swedish sentiment that grew in Norway towards the end of the century. At home he counted among his friends the dramatist and poet Henrik Ibsen, whom he engaged as the stage manager for his theatre, and Bjørnstjerne Bjørnson, who later became his director. Abroad he befriended Ralph Waldo Emerson, Henry Wadsworth Longfellow, who used him as a model for the musician in his *Tales of a Wayside Inn*, and Hans Christian Andersen, who made him the subject of one of his own stories.

Though hailed as Paganini's equal by Robert Schumann, no less, and as his superior by others, Bull was by no means universally admired. He divided opinion. One critic could write that he "has the bow of an angel in his hands. His instrument... becomes a human voice when he plays it and not a stringed instrument. If there were a blind person in the theatre, he would say that sometimes it was a clarinet, or a lute, or the sweetest voice of a nightingale". In 1858, the celebrated music critic, Eduard Hanslick, (himself the model for the character Beckmesser in Wagner's opera, *Die Meistersinger von Nürnberg*) wrote with admiration of Bull's harmonics and double stops, "both are executed with brilliant security and purity ... Still more brilliant are his staccatos, whch he renders unsurpassably, both up-bow and down-bow ... His tone has a beautiful softness". At the same time he spoke of Bull as "given to a one-sided virtuosity, to a combination of sovereign bravura and bizarre manners, which might be called 'Paganinic'. We demand of a virtuoso, himself insignificant as a composer, that he place his technical abilities at the service of superior music. Now, as he did 20 years ago, Ole Bull plays only his own compositions." Hanslick was not alone in this view; Bull's five-year-younger contemporary and fellow-countryman Halfdan Kjerulf, complained of the absence of serious music in his programmes.

Robert Schumann (1810-56) whose Piano Concerto Grieg heard in Leipzig and which inspired his own in A minor.

Chapter 3

Leipzig 1858-1862

On the occasion of his visit to Landås, Bull commanded, to use Grieg's own word, that the boy should be sent to the Leipzig Conservatoire, and his parents did not demur. The very same autumn saw his departure for the continent. One of his relatives had studied the piano there in the mid-1850s, and his father must have talked to him about the great German musical centre. Much has been made, not least by Grieg himself, of his unhappiness with its conservative musical ethos, and there is no doubt that the 15-year-old felt very much out of his depth, particularly during the first months of his stay. One of his father's friends accompanied him to Hamburg and then on to Leipzig, with its "tall, dark and gloomy houses and narrow streets", which almost took his breath away. He wept uncontrollably when his father's friend left. His sense of isolation was overwhelming. That farewell was the last time he was to hear his own language for several months, and he felt terribly homesick. He found the whole musical ethos of the place uncongenial: music stopped with Mendelssohn while his

Leipzig in the 1860s.

own idols, Chopin and Schumann, not to mention Wagner, were regarded as little short of subversive. Towards the end of his life he wrote of Leipzig in most unflattering terms in a letter to Gerhard Schjelderup: "In spite of its conservatory and its university, Leipzig never was and never will be a cultured city. The inhabitants of the city are by nature altogether too bourgeois and philistine for that." And he never ceased to claim that he left Leipzig as ignorant as when he came. "True," he told Aimar Grønvold, "I learned a bit, to be sure, but my own individuality was still a closed book to me". Leipzig certainly

The Leipzig Conservatory which Grieg attended from 1858-1862.

Clara Schumann at about the time Grieg heard her in Leipzig.

brought him into contact with great music and musicians. He fell completely under the spell of Schumann and was present to hear his widow, Clara Schumann, playing the A minor concerto, on which his own in the same key was to be modelled. Ernst Ferdinand Wenzel, with whom he studied the piano, introduced him to the wider Schumann repertory, and towards the end of his time there Grieg paid him the compliment of dedicating to him his very first opus, the *Four Piano Pieces*. He also went to the opera to hear Wagner's *Tannhäuser* which made so great an impact that he went back to see it no fewer than 14 times.

His lessons, on the other hand, did not inspire such enthusiasm: the sonatas of Clementi did not engage the young Norwegian's interest. Louis Plaidy, with whom he at first studied was furious when he came to class with his Clementi Sonata unprepared. He threw his music across the room and sent him packing to his lodgings. Grieg was outraged and stood his ground. He complained to Wenzel at this outburst, and was moved to another teacher. He had not been long in Leipzig before Grieg discovered that the musical education he had received in Bergen had not really prepared him to compete adequately with the gifted students that he was now encountering, and he threw himself into his studies with enormous ardour. Among the foreign youngsters was Edward Dannreuther, gifted as both a pianist and a scholar. Not only was he to champion Liszt and Wagner but he also became a noted interpreter of the Grieg concerto. Another fellow-student was Arthur Sullivan. Grieg wrote:

"Sullivan at once distinguished himself by his talent for composition, and for the advanced knowledge of instrumentation which he had acquired before he came to the Conservatorium. While still a student he wrote the music to Shakespeare's *Tempest*, a few bars of which he once wrote in my album, and which displays the practised hand of an old master."

Grieg did not have a great deal to do with Sullivan, but he did recall one occasion with special pleasure:

"It was during a performance of Mendelssohn's *St Paul*. We sat and followed the music with the score, and what a score! It was Mendelssohn's own manuscript, which Sullivan had succeeded in borrowing for the occasion from the Director of the Conservatorium, an intimate friend of Mendelssohn's. With what reverence we turned from one page to another! We were amazed at the clear, firm notes which so well expressed the ideas of the writer."

24

Carl Reinecke, Grieg's composition teacher and conductor of the Leipzig Gewandhaus Orchestra

Although Grieg may not have liked Leipzig, Leipzig liked Grieg. The young Norwegian may have poured obloquy and scorn on the city in his later years, but he seems to have made a good impression on everyone there. So much so that in his last year he was sent to Carl Reinecke for composition. Apart from being professor of composition at the conservatory and an enormously prolific composer to boot, Reinecke was also conductor of the Gewandhaus Orchestra for some years. It is also evident that his professors were far more liberal in their outlook than he gives us to believe. A glance at the examples of his counterpoint and harmony exercises reproduced in their book by Benestad and Schjelderup-Ebbe[2] will show that they tolerated some highly chromatic harmony.

Discussing why Grieg was so persistent in his denigration of his Leipzig training, John Horton wonders, in his *Master Musicians* book, whether there is not another and simpler explanation. He argues that the traumatic effects of the illness he contracted there and which dogged him all his life, may in fact be to blame – at least in part. For in the spring of 1860 Edvard was afflicted by an attack of pleurisy which resulted in a collapsed lung. For the remainder of his days he was plagued with respiratory problems and had to struggle through life on one lung. Alarmed by news of his illness, his mother came down to nurse the young 16-year-old and when he was fit enough to travel, took him back to Bergen. Given his feelings about Leipzig, the months spent in the blissful surroundings of his home must have been unsettling, its joys clouded by the dread of his return. When the time came to go back to Germany in the autumn, he did at least have his older brother for company. John was to study the cello there. However, the fact that his younger brother had preceded him to Leipzig, had already given rise to some sibling resentment.

Grieg's teachers in counterpoint included Ernst Friedrich Richter and Moritz Hauptmann, and the fruit of his classes can be seen in the Fugue in F minor that he wrote at the end of 1861. When Hauptmann heard it, he exclaimed *Sehr hübsch, sehr musikalisch!* (Very pretty, very musical!). If Keats spoke in the *Ode to a Grecian Urn* of heard melodies as sweet but "unheard melodies as sweeter", one must say that this really should go unheard. By no stretch of the imagination could it be called sweet. It is hardly likely that Grieg himself would be too pleased at seeing this student exercise put on to compact disc as it has been in recent years.

For Reinecke he had to compose a string quartet, for which he felt highly ill-prepared. However a three-movement piece in D minor, modelled on the Viennese masters resulted and was played in class. And whatever Grieg may have said himself, about this and his other juvenilia, he felt sufficiently pleased with the quartet to include it in a concert of his works when he returned to Bergen. Moreover his teachers at Leipzig spoke well of him in their final reports. For his piano teacher, Ignaz Moscheles, Grieg had much admiration – as well he might! Moscheles had been a friend of both Beethoven and Mendelssohn, and spent two decades teaching in London before moving to Leipzig in the 1840s. With him he studied the Beethoven sonatas as well as learning Moscheles' own *Études*. The great pianist spoke of Grieg's "special diligence": Wenzel himself referred to him as "a student very dear to me" and wrote of his "precise and far-reaching proficiency with a simple but nonetheless sensible and expressive delivery".

Grieg played his *Four Piano Pieces*, op. 1, at his final examination and the positive impression made on his Leipzig teachers was widely shared. C. F. Peters of Leipzig published

Ignaz Moscheles with whom Grieg studied the piano.

them the following year, along with the settings of Heine and Chamisso, op. 2, that he had composed at the conservatoire.

On his return home Grieg lost no time in putting on his début concert on 21 May 1862. With the support of family and friends the young composer, still 18 years old, rented the *Arbeiderforening* (The Trades' Union Hall) and mounted an ambitious programme. As a soloist he played Beethoven's *Pathétique* Sonata, three of the four Pieces op. 1, he had written in Leipzig, and some *Études* of Moscheles. He also took part in

Grieg's testimonial from Reinecke in 1862.

the Schumann Piano Quartet, op. 47, accompanied his own *Four Songs*, op. 2, and then there were the three D minor quartet movements he had composed for Reinecke. The concert did not go unnoticed and the event was reported in one of the city's leading papers, *Bergensposten*. His playing excited much critical praise particularly in the Schumann Piano Quartet, but it was his own music that caused the greatest stir: "as a composer Grieg seems to have a great future awaiting him". The whole of the next year was spent in Bergen, apart from a holiday trip to London and Paris with his father and brother during the summer of 1862. He petitioned the Ministry of Education for a scholarship but to no avail, and eventually borrowed funds from his father so as to continue his studies. The obvious centre for these was Copenhagen, with which he had been much taken when he had stayed there on his way home from Leipzig.

It was still natural for Norwegians to look to Copenhagen rather than Stockholm as a spiritual home. For so long Norway had been little more than an outlying province of Denmark, and it was natural for Norwegian artists and intellectuals to gravitate to the Danish capital. In 1863 Copenhagen was the undoubted centre of Scandinavian music. It was the largest centre of population in Scandinavia, numbering some 170,000 inhabitants. At the turn of the seventeenth and eighteenth centuries Stockholm could boast a population of only 70,000, New York a mere 60,000 and Paris 550,000. When Grieg was growing up, Bergen had only 25,000 inhabitants.

In Niels Gade Copenhagen could claim possession of the

Niels Gade, the leading Danish composer of the day.

leading Scandinavian composer of the day. Gade himself had enjoyed great success in Leipzig 20 years earlier. Mendelssohn had championed Gade's First Symphony, *På Sjølunds fagre sletter* (*On Sjøland's fair plains*) and his Overture *Echoes from Ossian*. On Mendelssohn's death, Gade, then only 30, succeeded him as conductor of the Gewandhaus Orchestra. In Stockholm there was no figure of comparable standing. By the 1860s Franz Berwald, the first name we think of nowadays, was only beginning to emerge from the shadows into which the Swedish musical establishment had banished him.

But Gade was not the only attraction on the musical horizon. Though he is less well-known abroad, Johann Peter Emilius Hartmann was the Grand Old Man of Danish music. Composer of the national opera, *Liden Kirsti*, as well as being Gade's father-in-law, Hartmann was a commanding figure at this time and Grieg's admiration for his music never faltered. There was also his Danish composer-friend from his Leipzig years, Christian Frederik Emil Hornemann. Their friendship was to endure through to the 1890s.

Musical considerations apart, there were other attractions that the metropolis exerted on the young Grieg. Copenhagen is not only Scandinavia's outpost to the south, it is also Europe's window on the north, and as a cultural meeting-point it presented a stimulus that neither Christiania (as Oslo was then known) nor Stockholm could have afforded. When Grieg first visited it, he found an active theatrical scene and a concert life that had not yet had time to blossom in Christiania. Apart from its more abundant musical vitality, Copenhagen was also a great literary centre, and thanks to their common language (Norwegian and Danish were to all intents and purposes the same), Bjørnson, Ibsen and other Norwegian writers like Jonas Lie, who are less known outside Scandinavia, were published there rather than in Norway.

But there were also ties of family and friendship that drew Grieg towards the Danish capital. Not least of these was his uncle, Herman Hagerup, who had sold up his estate, Haukeland in 1853 and returned from Bergen to settle in Denmark. He lived with his family at Søllerød not far from the capital. The charms of his daughter, Nina whom he would have known in childhood while they were living at Haukeland, were now beginning to cast their spell. Very little is known about Nina as a young girl and (to quote Audan Kayser, the Curator of the Grieg Museum) judging from early photographs she appears "rather timid and quite plain". She was now 18, vivacious in temperament and possessed a natural, albeit untrained, singing voice. In later years when he had established an international reputation Grieg was to spend almost as much time in Denmark as he did in his own country.

Chapter 4

Copenhagen

Although Grieg did not go to Copenhagen in 1863 specifically to study with Gade (the name means street in Danish), he must have hoped to have some guidance and perhaps tuition from him. Grieg met the Danish master quite by chance when taking a stroll in Klampenborg with his friend, Gottfried Mattison-Hansen, who introduced them. Later in life Grieg was at pains to stress that he had never taken any formal lessons but rather benefitted generally from the criticism and advice the Danish composer gave him. The outcome of their first meeting was an invitation to bring him some of his compositions. When Grieg

Copenhagen: Kongens Nytorv and the Royal Theatre, which houses both opera and drama.

KØBENHAVN   Kongens Nytorv

30

The Tivoli Gardens, Copenhagen where the last three movements of Grieg's symphony were first performed under H.C.Lumbye in 1865.

went along a few days later, he showed him some early piano pieces and the Songs op. 2. At the corresponding stage in his career, Gade was writing ambitious large-scale orchestral pieces and had already made his breakthrough with the C minor Symphony, so this must have seemed small beer. He did not disguise a certain impatience with these trifles. No doubt he felt that the young man showed a certain want of creative ambition, and needed to flex his muscles. Up to a point he was right, for he must have sensed that the young Norwegian was far from confident of his powers at this stage. Gade urged him to try his hand at something big – a symphony. Grieg rose to the challenge and had the first movement ready and fully scored within a fortnight. But it was a further year before the work was completely finished. Only the last three movements were played at the première in June 1864. This took place a couple of weeks before Grieg's 21st birthday at a concert in Tivoli, Copenhagen's delightful pleasure gardens. The three movements were conducted by H. C. Lumbye, the so-called "Johann Strauss of the North", famous for his popular *Champagne Galop*. The complete Symphony was given for the first time in Grieg's native city, Bergen the following season and

31

then again in 1867. Grieg himself conducted the two inner movements in Copenhagen in 1865 and the last three in Christiania in 1867.

But then something extraordinary happened. Not long after presenting the three movements from his symphony in Christiania, Grieg attended a concert in which his countryman Johan Svendsen conducted his own First Symphony in D major. To Grieg, Svendsen's symphony came as a revelation. It, too, was a student work but it has much greater personality and assurance than Grieg's. In the Christiania daily, *Aftenbladet,* he called it a work of "scintillating genius, superb national feeling and truly brilliant handling of the orchestra... Everything had my fullest sympathy and forced itself upon me with irresistible power". Its excellence made him more than ever aware of the deficiences of his own piece. And he came to the decision that he must withdraw it.

Three years older than Grieg, Svendsen had grown up in Christiania with music all round him. His father was a bandmaster and by the time Johan was 15, he was already an accomplished violinist, and played the flute and clarinet as well. As with Grieg, Svendsen's musical schooling was in Leipzig, where he was enrolled in 1864. He studied the violin under Ferdinand David and composition with Reinecke. It was in Leipzig that he wrote his first works, a Quartet in A minor, op. 1, some choral pieces, and at the end of his two years of study, the captivating Octet for strings, op.3. Svendsen found himself very early on and even his early works speak with an individual voice. Indeed his Leipzig years were both happier and more fruitful than Grieg's, and the Octet, the First Symphony, op.4, and the String Quintet, op.5, are all works of astonishing individuality, assurance and, above all, freshness. After finishing his studies in Leipzig and returning to Norway, he undertook a long tour in 1867 embracing Scotland, Iceland and the Færoes, returning to Christiania to conduct his symphony later in the year. For the remainder of the 1860s, Svendsen lived in Paris, ekeing out a living as an orchestral player and working on his Violin Concerto. In 1870 at the outbreak of the Franco-Prussian war, he moved to Leipzig acting for a time as leader and conductor of the Euterpe Concert Society. He spent the following summer in Bayreuth where he was much in the company of Wagner. His best-known and most brilliant score is *Carnival in Paris,* op. 9 (1872), which was begun in New York, continued in Leipzig and finished in Bayreuth. This was an evocation of the festive processions that he recalled from his time in Paris, "the most glorious city on earth" he called it. But

Johan Severin Svendsen,
composer and conductor.

by the 1870s Svendsen had given up the violin owing to problems with his left hand and by this time he had been drawn into the Liszt–Wagner circle. Later in life, he was to introduce *Die Walküre* and *Siegfried*, among other things, to the Copenhagen operatic public. He returned to Norway for a short time but in 1877 gave up the direction of the Christiania Orchestra, which he had shared with Grieg, becoming more of what we would now call a "star" conductor, appearing in London, Paris, Leipzig and other great musical centres.

Svendsen was a master of the orchestra, for which in his youth Grieg had no particular flair. He could think in longer musical paragraphs and his symphony shows an astonishing confidence and inventiveness. Even though he and Grieg were good friends, Svendsen was never to involve himself in the folksong movement to anywhere near the same extent as did Grieg: the *Four Norwegian Rhapsodies* were probably as close as he ever came to it. But there is still a distinctively Norwegian feel to his melodic ideas. Alas, the creative fires burnt themselves out not long after he settled in Copenhagen, and after the famous *Romance in G major* for violin and orchestra, he more or less gave up composing.

But for all his admiration for the Svendsen's symphony, Grieg thought sufficiently well of the inner movements of his own to arrange them for piano-duet, publishing them in 1869 as *Two Symphonic Pieces*, op.14. In a letter to his Leipzig publisher, C. F. Peters he wrote, "I heard them played many years ago in Copenhagen. They sounded pretty good but I would not for all the world publish the orchestral score now because this work belongs to a vanished Schumann period from my life." Performances of the complete symphony remained under embargo for the remainder of Grieg's lifetime and until quite recently. When he bequeathed the score to the Bergen Public Library, Grieg was quite adamant about the piece: "*Må aldrig opføres*" (Must never be performed!) was the injunction he scrawled on the title-page. But then a photocopy of the autograph score was surreptitiously spirited off to the then Soviet Union and played on Moscow Radio so that the case for upholding Grieg's ban went by default. It was performed at the 1981 Bergen Festival and immediately recorded, and the score published three years later in the Collected Edition of Grieg's Works (*Grieg Gesamtausgabe*).

In the congenial atmosphere of Copenhagen his spirits flourished and his musical activities prospered. In July 1864, Edvard and Nina had become engaged despite the opposition of both their parents. Incest and the fear of its consequences, haunted Nordic society in the nineteenth century in almost the same way as AIDS or drug addiction do in our own times, and the prospect of a marriage between cousins would have prompted concern. But their kinship was not the only grounds for anxiety. Nina's mother wrote in no uncertain (and comically unprophetic) terms of her future son-in-law: "He is nothing and he has nothing and he writes music that nobody wants to listen to!" Edvard's father was hardly more encouraging though he naturally took a more percipient view as to his son's prospects. Eventually their hostility subsided sufficiently for them to be allowed to make their engagement public, though it was a long time before it completely abated.

Nina herself was already quite an accomplished singer, and Grieg celebrated their bethrothal with the *Six Songs*, op. 4, to German texts, poems by Chamisso, Heine and Uhlund. These appeared with a dedication "to Fräulein Nina Hagerup". In their harmonies and general sound world they very much resemble Schumann but they show the young composer developing a bolder and imaginative style of his own. He also ventured into Danish for the first time with his settings of Christian Winther, published as op.10, and more impressively with the four *Hjertets Melodier (Melodies of the heart)* to poems of Hans Christian Andersen. Known outside Denmark mainly for his children's stories, Hans Christian Andersen was a considerable poet. Grieg had only recently met the famous writer, which no doubt acted as a further spur, and two of his settings, *Jeg elsker Dig (I love thee)*[3] and *To brune Øine (Two brown eyes)*, won a celebrity that proved both immediate and enduring.

When Grieg had returned to Bergen for the summer holidays in July 1864, he had spent some time with Ole Bull at his home at Valestrand, not far from the city. "Ole Bull introduced me", as Grieg put it in a conversation in Berlin in 1907 with the American writer, Arthur Abell, to the "trollish Norwegian melodies that so strongly fascinated me, and awakened the desire to have them as the basis for my own melodies". Bull brought him into contact with some of the best *spillemen* (fiddlers) whose strong character inspired him. "Had it not been for Ole Bull, I would have written colourless music à la Gade. He slavishly imitated Mendelssohn of whom he was only a pale echo. 'Edvard,' he said, 'this is not the path you are destined to follow. Throw off Gade's yoke. Create your own style! You have it in you. Write music that will bring honour to your own land. You must develop a strong Norwegian sound world. You can become famous if you do that, but if you follow

Rikard Nordraak, Grieg's friend and the composer of the Norwegian national anthem, *Ja vi elsker dette landet*.

in Gade's footsteps you will only founder in the mire.'"

Later the same year brought with it another encounter that was to prove equally fateful both for Grieg in particular and for Norwegian music in general. Back in Copenhagen he met another Norwegian, Rikard Nordraak, an ardent spirit whose promise was to be cruelly cut short only two years later. The two youngsters were to spend much of their time in each other's company during this period and it was Nordraak who alerted Grieg to the enormous creative potential represented by Norwegian folk music. Lindeman's collection of *Ældre og Nyere Norske Fjeldmelodier* (*Older and Newer Norwegian Mountain Melodies*) had fired the imagination of many Norwegian musicians since their first appearance in 1853, but none more than Nordraak.

His meeting with Nordraak kindled Grieg's enthusiam for this folk heritage. "Listen" Nordraak once wrote, "to the unclothed plaintive melodies that wander, like so many orphans, round the countryside all over Norway. Gather them about you... and let them tell you their stories. Remember them all, reflect and then play each one afterwards so that you solve all the riddles and everyone thinks you like his story best." There was no more willing listener than Grieg.

Nordraak is an enigmatic figure. He composed the tune, *Ja, vi elsker dette Landet* (*Yes, we love this land*), which was to become Norway's national anthem, to words by his cousin, Bjørnstjerne Bjørnson. Had Nordraak lived, he might have enriched Norwegian music in other ways, even if his technique was vulnerable and his musical schooling far from finished. Although he was half-Danish, his allegiance to Norway, and all things Norwegian, was uncompromising, and his captivating national fervour cast a spell that held Grieg and many others in its thrall. Nordraak did not have a modest opinion of his own talent and was (to quote John Horton) "impatient of technical discipline". He showed something of the arrogance one so often finds in the self-taught and the dilettante.

His is a puzzling reputation. Had he not met Grieg and their fates not been briefly intertwined, it is open to question as to whether he would have made any significant mark on Norway's musical history. None of his 40-odd pieces has made any inroads into the wider musical repertory. It is not unreasonable to speak of Nordraak as a composer of promise rather than fulfilment. To be fair, Nils Grinde in his *History of Norwegian music* (Oslo, 1971), speaks of him as "bearing the marks of an inexperienced composer", but goes on to say that his best work "bears witness to an astonishing maturity and indicate that his artistic personality was already clearly defined. Of Grieg's contemporaries he is the only one whose style is independent of Grieg's. He had not only developed more quickly but in an entirely different direction."

In the summer of 1866 Grieg had met Halfdan Kjerulf for the first time. Kjerulf was then in his early fifties and the leading Norwegian song composer of the day. When Grieg had spoken of his enthusiasm for Nordraak, Kjerulf had exclaimed with alarm, "Well, I must say! *Les extremes se touchent!*" (Opposites are drawn to each other.) Be this as it may, Grieg found enormous stimulus and inspiration in Nordraak's company. As he later told his younger countryman, the composer Iver Holter, "Nordraak's influence on me is not exaggerated. It really is so: through him and only through him was I truly awakened".

In 1865 the two friends had planned to spend the autumn and winter in Italy, the country beloved of all Scandinavians, where the climate was more relaxing and where the cost of living cheaper. But instead of staying in Copenhagen during the summer of 1865 Nordraak decided to go on to Berlin ("that disgusting hole", Grieg called it) where he thought he had found a teacher that suited him. Grieg remained in Denmark but by the time he arrived in Berlin in early October, Nordraak was intent on staying put. A fortnight later he was in bed with pneumonia and unfit to travel even had he wanted to. Judging from an early letter it would seem that Grieg had not realised the gravity of Nordraak's condition. The doctor diagnosed a severe jaundice as well as pneumonia and pleurisy, and among other things, prescribed six leeches for a three-hour bleeding! By the beginning of November the worst seemed to be over, and Grieg left for Leipzig to appear in two concerts that the conservatoire was presenting at the Gewandhaus. He promised to return for him in a few days.

The concerts, at which he presented the Piano Sonata in E minor, op. 7, and the Violin Sonata No. 1 in F major, op. 8 which he had composed in Denmark were a great success. It was here that he first met his countryman, Johan Svendsen who was approaching the last year of studies at the conservatoire, and whose First Symphony was to make such an impression on him.

In Berlin Nordraak impatiently awaited his friend's return, and his letter pleading with Grieg to come back makes poignant reading. By the end of the month Grieg had decided to break his promise and go on to Rome with another travelling companion. Nordraak gives vent to his sense of betrayal and despair in this letter written at the end of November, when at last he had given up hope of Grieg's return.

My dear Grieg!

After being made a fool of for a whole month, I have now learned for certain from your latest and, indeed, welcome letter that you are not coming here. I couldn't dream of being angry about this; on the contrary, since you have found a good travelling companion, I think the most reasonable thing you can do is to leave immediately for Italy and let Germany and its tight-fisted music publishers go to the devil. But what is and will always be a puzzle to me is the manner in which you have treated me since you left, and which, mildly speaking, I find contemptible toward someone that you call a friend, someone who was abandoned as you abandoned me; and I must say, of all the people I know, you are the last that I would have believed capable of such behaviour... If the reason for your silence was that you didn't want to say to me what you have said to others – namely, that you were not returning here – it was in the highest degree dishonest and cowardly; only at the beginning could I regard that as the thoughtfulness of a gentle spirit who didn't want to disappoint a sick man. But at the very least it was your duty, after you had given me your solemn promise, to let me know as soon as possible, either directly or indirectly. When you left, you said you were going to be gone, only a few days the result, naturally, was that I lay and waited day after day for your arrival .

You must excuse me, Grieg; know that I still think of you with deep affection. But my affection is burdened by a whole month's exasperation – the things that I have just told you, things that you, if you are thinking properly, will see have their basis and justification. And, dear Grieg, my beloved friend, I am afraid... that one fine day it will all be over... Never have I been in greater danger than now."

Most commentators have condemned Grieg out-of-hand, and one cannot view his abandonment of Nordraak without shame. Not that he was entirely negligent. He wrote to Nordraak on 6 November, shortly after his arrival in Leipzig and again a week later, and he telegraphed asking after his health a few days later. But Benestad and Schjelderup-Ebbe add one important rider that must qualify any precipitate rush to make any moral judgment. Grieg's own health was far from strong and the fear of further infection may well have played its part in his decision to break his word and not return to Berlin.

Chapter 5

Rome

Travel in the mid-1860s was a strenuous affair.[5] Grieg left Leipzig on 2 December by train and stayed briefly in Vienna where he heard a Lortzing opera and a Suppé operetta, and then travelled on to Venice. He describes Padua, Ferrara and Bologna and Pisa, and the absurdly rigorous customs examination including a body search in Civitavecchia and "being smoked" (or disinfected) for cholera. (This was not an uncommon precaution and the programme for a City of Birmingham Orchestra's concert when Sibelius visited it in 1921 noted that the Theatre Royal is "regularly disinfected throughout by the General Health Disinfecting Company".) These were the years before the unification of Italy had been completed. Austria was the dominant power in the north, and the French still maintained a presence there. The provinces of Italy, Piedmont, the Veneto, Tuscany and so on, were independent entities or alternatively Austrian protectorates. Grieg arrived in the eternal city on the 11 December and began devouring the sights. This first stay in Rome is well documented for the composer kept a diary recording his impressions, very different from the concise and purely factual record of events that mark other periods of his life such as the last three years (1905–7). They do not bring Grieg alive before our eyes in the same way as do his letters. It is obvious from the letters that Grieg was blessed with the great gifts of both giving his friendship and attracting the devotion and friendship of others. He maintained, as people did in those years, a long, obviously time-consuming correspondence with friends, into which he poured much energy. Grieg was a wonderfully natural writer – and he was an accomplished, highly articulate speaker. But the diary entries for his Roman visit are vivid. One graphically describes a nocturnal visit to the Colosseum on New Year's Eve:

The Colosseum in 1855.

"In the evening a wonderful moonlit tour to the Forum Romanum. This is the right environment in which to view the ruins. The impact of the Colosseum is indescribable. The French watchman who guards all the entrances used only a lantern to inspect all the gates and arches. The reddish light reflecting off the old arches and shining in among the ruins created an interesting contrast to the strange half-darkness produced by the blue-green light of the moon and made the whole scene even more ghostly. ... The moon shone so pale and cold, our imagination began to play tricks on us, and we hurried as fast as we could away from this admittedly romantic but nonetheless unpleasant world where assaults are anything but rare. Next we went to the Scandinavian Society to celebrate New Year's Eve, but it was so formal and uncomfortable in this "homey circle" that after staying for only five minutes or so, and without telling anybody, I just left. We drank our chocolate in the Café Greco and talked about our loved ones at home. By 11 o'clock I was sound asleep." (excerpt from Grieg's diary, 31 December)

The following day he and some fellow countrymen went on a hike in the country:

"At 9.30 in the morning I and a group of other Norwegians gathered in Café Roma to make a hike in the Campagna. We went through Porta St Sebastiano on the old Roman highway in the most enormous heat – roughly like a July day at home. We had breakfast at a little restaurant outdoors; the meal consisted of a dirty sausage and dirty spare ribs on even dirtier plates, and some most undrinkable wine, but even so it was a singular delight. The mere thought that on the first of January – under beautiful green trees, and surrounded by the scent of roses – I was sitting out in the open air and eating my breakfast, made me almost intoxicated. From here we walked… under the dark blue sky and in the shimmering summer air toward the indescribably beautiful Alban Hills that lay in the distance. Hans Christian Andersen is right: Italy is the land of colour. The light, clear air gives a wonderful harmony to the colours. The mountains look like dust, like ether, like things that are merely hovering in one's thoughts, and yet in such a way that one sees and enjoys all of this with one's outer as well as one's inner eye."

Henrik Ibsen, the great Norwegian playwright, in the early 1860s.

Grieg often spent his free time at the Scandinavian Society, and it was here that he met Henrik Ibsen, the greatest Norwegian of his age, the poet Andreas Munch and other artists. Ibsen was some 15 years older than Grieg, being born in 1828 in the country town of Skien, which had once served as Norway's capital. He had left Norway in 1864, and apart from a couple of visits, remained abroad for the next 27 years. His absence was not solely because of the more congenial climate and life-style of Italy and the continent, but arose from disgust at Norway's failure to give any support to Denmark during the short war with Prussia that took place in 1864. Ibsen had warned against the Prussian threat and while he was in Berlin on his way south, he had witnessed the triumphal return of the Prussian army after the Danish defences at the border town of Dybbøl had fallen. His disillusion is well expressed in a letter to Bjørnson in which he spoke of the need to put to an end the romanicization of our ancient history because "present Norwegians have as little as common with the old ones as the Greek pirates have with the generation which sailed to Troy". At this time Ibsen was working on his early masterpiece, *Brand*, which was published in March 1866 and marked his breakthrough. In the wake of its success, he embarked on *Peer Gynt* with which Grieg was to be so deeply involved. On Christmas Eve there was always a celebration at the Society and on this occasion Grieg heard a talk by Ibsen; the following day there was an informal "feast on the leftovers ... [at which he saw] Ibsen dead drunk". Grieg was far from uncritical of the Roman establishment as can be seen from this diary entry of 17 February 1866:

"We walked out to St Paul's Church, this elegant building that in some respects even surpasses St Peter's... When one hears that this enormous church exists only for show, one cannot help asking the question: where on earth does all the money come from, for as everyone knows the country is anything but rich! Ah yes, the people are coerced into paying tax to this enormous church because that is pleasing to God! It is a terrible illusion that the worship of God consists in building majestic temples that must, indeed, be admired – but for the sake of which the people sigh in bondage and misery."

A visit to St Peter's, some weeks later compounded his astonishment:

"Such a thing I had never dreamt of. My imagination could never venture to create such a poetic, stupid, and colossal picture. The

Rome 1860 –
The Vatican
Library.

whole church was a sea of fire, even the cross above the dome, so it is
no wonder that the man [a prisoner] who is assigned to place the
lamps in this dizzying height, always takes the sacrament of
communion before he climbs up. But the thing about this that must
not only astonish but outrage every thinking person is that people
think they can please God by such nonsense."

Some commentators have spoken of his naïveté on political
matters, perhaps with reason, but one diary entry (16 March
1866) strikes resonances nearer home. Certainly he was a
republican by sentiment and his sympathies were on the side of
the underdog and not the privileged. In later life he was to refer
to Christiania as "a nest of Tories", but although he was
strongly nationalist in feeling, he was fully conscious of the
dangers of unbridled nationalism.

"Later I became convinced in a new and sad way that Rome is the
ruins of a vanished greatness, and that is all. It is dangerous for a
people – both with respect to politics and with respect to art – to have
a great past. It leads either to what the Germans are sinking into,
namely striving with all their might to hold themselves up, and with

44

this striving to produce nothing but artificial, baroque, unnatural things; or else, as here among the Romans, quite phlegmatically to lull themselves to sleep and rest on their laurels."

Grieg's thoughts must have often turned to Nordraak but he must have been unprepared for the grave tidings that were to come. He was thunderstruck by the news of Nordraak's death when it eventually reached him in Rome on 6 April 1866. Given the way he had abandoned his friend, his grief must have been compounded with a terrible sense of guilt. He marked the date with a cross in his diary. "the most dreadful blow that I could have received – Nordraak is dead! he, my only dearest friend, our great hope for our Norwegian art".[6] Not that he blamed himself entirely. He always maintained that had Nordraak kept to their original plan and left in October, and not stayed on in Berlin, he might never have contracted his fatal illness. On his homeward journey he visited Nordraak's grave in Berlin and wrote a touching letter of condolence to his father. He also composed a piece in his memory, *Sorgemarsj til minne om Rikard Nordraak* (*Funeral March for Rikard Nordraak*), for piano, arranging it for wind and percussion the following year. Incidentally, such were the resonances of this event that he asked for it to be played at his own funeral, and indeed it was when the time finally came in September 1907.

The only other composition of note from his Italian stay was the Concert Overture, *I Høst* (*In Autumn*). Apart from the symphony, this was his first work for orchestra. It derives its melodic inspiration from the song, '*Efteraarsstormen*' ('*Autumn storm*') to words of Christian Richardt. This he had written the previous year, including it in his Op. 18 collection of 1869. In assessing it we are handicapped by the fact that the orchestral score does not survive in its original form. We know it only in the revision Grieg made 20 years later in 1887, by which time he had acquired much greater expertise in writing for the orchestra. It is probable that he had the example of Gade's first orchestral work, the *Echoes from Ossian* Overture in mind, and expected that it would put him on the map in much the same way that Gade's piece had established the Danish master. But when he showed him the score on his return from Italy, Gade was far from enthusiastic. In later years Grieg recalled that Gade called the piece rubbish and told him to "go home and write something better". Grieg told Iver Holter that the piece was badly orchestrated but at the time he was so upset by Gade's dismissive response, that he put it to one side. All the same he believed in it enough to make a piano-duet transcription, which he and Nina played. And he must have felt sufficiently pleased with it to submit it for a competition sponsored by the Royal Swedish Academy of Music the following year. The judges were Julius Rietz from Dresden, the Swedish composer August Söderman and Gade himself – and to Grieg's delight, his piece won first prize! Even so it must be conceded that even in its 1887 orchestration, the *In Autumn* Overture is not one of Grieg's strongest pieces.

It is evident on his return from Rome to Denmark in May 1866 that during their separation, a certain *froideur* had developed between Edvard and his fiancée, for reasons which are not at all clear. In some way this was prophetic of their future marriage which was far from untroubled. It may have been largely successful but there were long periods of turbulence. While he had been in Italy, Nina had spent a few months in Bergen with his parents. They were not much of a success. Grieg records her return to Denmark in casual, matter-of-fact terms in his diary. A letter from his Danish friend Benjamin Feddersen refers to Nina in critical terms, which he would not have dared to do had their relations been wholly harmonious. He obviously sees her as unworthy of him. "How I regard Miss Hagerup I would prefer to say to her directly. I am sorry that she has not understood her relationship with you; for no matter how much you may wish to excuse her I still maintain that she is not the woman who deserves to support and encourage you in the development of your talent." Grieg himself makes very few other references to her in his diary. The Hagerup family had never been particularly keen on the match, preferring a husband of means rather than aspirations. As Feddersen put it, "all they require for their daughter is a man, preferably a rich one, whose life is assured for 100 years".

Faced with the prospect of supporting himself and a future wife Grieg's thoughts turned to the practicalities of life and he set about getting a musical position. A conducting post in the theatre at Christiania would do – and to this end he enlisted the help of Ibsen and Bjørnson. The great dramatist was in no doubt as to Grieg's talent, as his reply shows. "Don't be angry with Bjørnson," Ibsen told him when he complained that a letter to him had gone unanswered. "Write to him once more... tell him that they must let you have the position. Tell him that you have a right to it." But Ibsen's letter had been long in coming and by the time it had, the position had been filled. A second possibility was to prepare himself as a cathedral organist. He took a number of lessons from his friend Gottfried

Matthison-Hansen and spent much of his summer practising the instrument. It was Matthison-Hansen, who had introduced him to Gade and whose father was organist of Roskilde Cathedral. Grieg finally went to Roskilde and played some Bach pieces for him including the G minor Fugue. Much to his satisfaction, he was furnished with a testimonial that was generous in its praises. However, fortunately for posterity, Grieg's career took a different course and his ambitions for a cathedral post either in Denmark or Norway soon petered out.

Chapter 6

Bergen and Marriage

Grieg returned to Bergen in September 1866 after an absence of two years and gave a concert there on 3 October in which he played some of the *Humoresques*, and the Piano Sonata in E minor, op. 7. Early the following month he moved to Christiania, which was to remain his base for the next ten years. On 15 October he gave another recital in the banqueting room of the Hotel du Nord, repeating the *Humoresques*, three movements of the Sonata, and accompanying Wilhelmine Norman Neruda in his F major Sonata, op. 8. *Aftenbladet*'s review the following day mentioned that "his fame had

Wilhelmine Norman Neruda, the violinist whom Grieg accompanied in his F major Sonata, op. 8.

preceded him", and the fact that he was joined by Norman Neruda testifies to this. She was one of the most celebrated virtuosi of her day, and was married at this time to the Swedish composer, conductor and pianist, Ludvig Norman with whom she travelled widely.

Nina came to Norway for the concert and sang the op. 5 settings, *Hjertets Melodier* (*Songs of the Heart*) as well as some songs by Kjerulf and Nordraak. It is clear from a letter to Matthison-Hansen that the success of the concert, which must have been enhanced by the violinist's celebrity gave him greater faith in himself. "Relations with Nina's parents", he told Mathison-Hansen, "have been foul, so stay away from them – though I think things have been better of late because of a very successful concert I gave here with the help of Mrs Norman and my fiancée, both of whom were in Norway recently. You should have heard Mrs Norman play the violin sonata! I tell you, I hardly knew whether I should keep on playing or just stop and listen to her! The concert included nothing but Norwegian music(!) ... and has given me courage and confidence in the future." The concert was a great critical success: *Aftenbladet's* review ran to no fewer than 6,500 words, long then and unthinkable now! Otto Winter-Hjelm, a friend and colleague, wrote that the F major sonata, op. 8, suffered from the influence of Gade which may be "beneficial with respect to form but injurious when it comes to content". Having no job either as conductor or organist, Grieg settled on teaching and together with Winter-Hjelm, he decided to found a music academy. Ole Bull had made such a suggestion some years earlier in 1862 and Winter-Hjelm had started a more rudimentary school two years later. But the musical academy proper came into being early in 1867 with a small staff and with Winter-Hjelm and Grieg teaching theory and score reading, and Grieg also teaching the piano.

By this time Grieg was making ends meet sufficiently to consider marriage to Nina despite the continued opposition of their respective families. Indeed when the ceremony was eventually performed, at the Johanneskirke in Copenhagen on 11 June 1867, only friends were present. Grieg's relations with his own parents were far from untroubled at this time. They were as unenthusiastic about Nina as her parents were about him. Even though Nina had stayed some months in Bergen while Edvard had been in Italy, there was little warmth in her relations with her future parents-in-law. Nor was much love lost between Gesine, Grieg's mother and Nina's parents – and in particular her mother. Grieg's correspondence with his family was tinged with acrimony at this period. Generally speaking, the young composer's growing self-confidence may have fostered impatience. In a letter written some weeks after the marriage, Alexander upbraided his son for his arrogance. In any event relations were sufficiently strained for them not to go to Copenhagen for the wedding, hardly a matter for surprise since they had not been invited. Grieg's father was obviously distressed. "Believe me, it pains me that I am not able to be present at your wedding... You will certainly not be surprised that I am staying away, since I have not heard either from you or from anyone a word to the effect that I or any of the family

A Grieg family portrait at Landås in the 1860s: in the backrow from left to right, Grieg's sisters, Maren and Elisabeth, and his wife Nina; in the middle his father Alexander, brother John, his mother Gesine and the composer himself; seated Grieg's cousin, Marianne Riis, John's wife Marie, and Grieg's sister Benedictine.

would be welcome at your and Nina's marriage."

The young couple were nothing if not even-handed for Nina's parents were not invited either. They had never been particularly fond of or welcoming to Edvard since their betrothal. At least when the bridal pair returned to Christiania there was some softening in the attitude of Grieg's parents. There were conciliatory letters waiting at Øvre Voldgate 2, their new home and soon some possessions, furniture, a piano and so on, which Grieg's mother had promised them. The congratulatory letters were not wholly without a gentle touch of malice. Grieg's sister, Elisabeth wrote that she would try to stop remembering Nina "as a drill sergeant". Nina must have been a spirited young lady. Like her husband she was small of stature, and in later years both were to refer to themselves as "the trolls".

Nor were Grieg's relations with his brother particularly harmonious either, although he had composed an Intermezzo in A minor (CW118) for him only a few months earlier, in 1866. John's attitude towards his brother was clouded by resentment. His musical ambitions had had to take second place to filial obligations. By the mid-1860s he was in the family business, and for many years still nourished symptoms of sibling rivalry. Although he was the older of the two brothers, it had been Edvard who had been chosen to go to Lepizig, long before he was given the opportunity. Understandable though this may seem to us from the vantage point of posterity, from his perspective in Bergen in the late 1850s–early 1860s, it must have seemed very different. Obvious though it was to others (and certainly to Ole Bull) that Edvard's was the superior talent, this was not how he saw it! The tension that developed between the two brothers persisted for some little while, long after Grieg and his father were reconciled. Fortunately the latter lived long enough to see it resolved by the early 1870s.

1867 was a difficult year in other respects. Grieg's teaching duties were burdensome and inhibited composition though there was one glimmer of light, his collaboration with Svendsen who was now back in Norway. Both he and Svendsen gave concerts during the autumn, each devoted entirely to their own music. Svendsen's, on 12 October included the performance of the D major Symphony, which Grieg reviewed in *Aftenbladet* in extravagent terms and which led, as we have seen, to the subsequent withdrawal of his own symphony. Grieg's concert included three new compositions; the G major violin sonata, op. 13, which he had written earlier that summer in the immediate wake of his honeymoon, a gavotte for violin and piano and some choruses.

At this stage in his life he composed hardly anything during term-time – for apart from teaching, he was also active as conductor of the Philharmonic Society. However the Philharmonic Society was dissolved in the spring of 1868, and Grieg formed his own orchestra. They gave four concerts in all and their programmes seem very safe, tame choices from our present-day vantage point. To an audience as unsophisticated as that of the Norwegian capital, however, what would have been staple diet on the continent or in England was fresh and unfamiliar – Beethoven's Fifth Symphony, Mozart's G minor (No. 40), and nearer home, Gade's oratorio, *Korsfarerne* (*The Crusaders*). The standard was such as to call for tolerance ("I need only note that the orchestra is dreadful. They all crash and bang as if their lives depended on it", wrote Grieg in a letter to Matthison-Hansen, 18 March 1868). However the section-leaders were a good deal more experienced as players than he was as a conductor.

Grieg who had begun his conducting career in Copenhagen in 1865 may have felt confident that he was, as he said in an earlier letter, a "conductor par excellence". Whether or not he meant this ironically, his musicians certainly took a different view. The orchestra comprised some 18 strings, some of whom were amateurs though the wind players were drawn from the theatre orchestra. Even later on in the 1870s Grieg's technique was still not fully developed and his rehearsal methods certainly left some room for improvement. When rehearsing Schumann's *Paradise and the Peri*, instead of concentrating on those episodes that posed problems and explaining what he wanted, he would merely ask his musicians to go over the offending passages again. This naturally exasperated his players. At the end when he merely asked, "Once more from the beginning, please", his leader, Fredrik Ursin brought down the house by saying "That's all we need" and then immediately breaking into a dance tune! Moreover during the very first season in 1867-68 there had been some ill-feeling over money. Grieg had managed to keep the concerts afloat and even made a profit but was criticised for keeping the money himself instead of sharing it out with his musicians.

Not long after their marriage Nina became pregnant and April 1868 brought the couple good fortune – the birth of a daughter, Alexandra. The young parents were in transports of delight, and it was the news of this event that brought about a reconciliation with his father. To be fair, it is the father who again took the initiative and whose letters are the more conciliatory in tone. He possessed a generosity of spirit which his son inherited but was slow to exhibit during their estrangement in 1866. Indeed the youthful arrogance and conceit of which Edvard's father complained, was posing problems in Christiania's musical world, and undermining the good will which the young composer needed. He was working very hard, giving lessons for very little money and was impatient of the constraints and limitations of musical life in the Norwegian capital.

With term-time over, summer offered the only solace and escape for the creative work in which Grieg so longed to immerse himself. The young family left Christiania and repaired to Denmark; Nina and the baby stayed in Copenhagen

Grieg's autograph of
the Piano Concerto.

with her parents while Grieg rented a small place in Søllerød in
Zeeland where he could work undisturbed. It was here that he
began the Piano Concerto in A minor, a project furthered by
the presence in a villa nearby of Edmund Neupert, the leading
Norwegian pianist of the day. It was a very hot summer but he
worked hard and always looked back on those weeks as "halcyon
days". It is worth a reminder that it was only the piano part and
a rough outline of the orchestral accompaniment in short score
that was finished in Søllerød – not the whole piece as is
occasionally asserted.

On his return to Christiania that autumn he settled back
into his daily routine of teaching and conducting. He longed to
finish scoring the concerto, though the obstacles of rehearsals,

giving lessons and generally making ends meet, slowed down its progress and heightened his frustration. The projected first performance in Copenhagen had to be postponed and when it eventually did take place, the 25-year-old Grieg was too overwhelmed with duties in Christiania to witness its triumph.

It was on 3 April, 1869 that Eduard Neupert sent the concerto into its international orbit. It was a glittering occasion. Not only was the Queen of Denmark present, but such musical notables as Niels Gade and J.P.E. Hartmann. No less a pianistic luminary than Anton Rubinstein, who was on tour in Denmark, actually lent the grand piano with which he travelled for the occasion. Not only was each movement enthusiastically applauded but applause broke out even after the first movement cadenza! The concerto has never lost its capacity to take one by surprise by its perennial freshness and invention. Every commentator mentions its obvious debt to Schumann's concerto in the same key, which had made such "an indelible impression" on Grieg when he heard Clara Schumann playing it during his Leipzig days, but no one disputes its total originality. When at long last Neupert played it in Christiania the following August, it was hailed by the critic of *Aftenbladet* as "new, original and inspired," and such it remains today. However, the version the Danish and Norwegian audiences heard was different from the one familiar to us today. Given its lyrical appeal, it seems incredbile that two publishers turned it down, and it was only thanks to Svendsen's insistent recommendation that the publisher Fritsch changed his mind. It eventually appeared in print, albeit three years later. But throughout his life, Grieg remained unhappy with both the solo and orchestral part and constantly returned to the task of revision. Plans for a second concerto in 1883-84 came to nothing. The first published score, which already embodied some changes gives the second subject to a solo trumpet and not to the cellos, a suggestion emanating from Liszt whom Grieg met in Rome in 1870, a year after the first performance. Grieg made the final revision as late as 1906-07, the last year of his life.

Grieg himself included the concerto on many of his tours and the work has remained one of the most popular works in the repertoire. Yet such is the quality and profusion of ideas in the Concerto that it survives unceasing exposure in the concert halls of the world unscathed only to emerge with renewed and seemingly indescructible freshness. Grieg was never to become a master of large-scale structures. His friend Svendsen had a much stronger feeling for form. But as John Horton points out,

Anton Rubinstein,
pianist and composer.

the Piano Concerto is never completely subservient to form and offers "a bold admixture of Lisztian bravura and a happy blend of his own inborn harmonic originality with the national colouring he had been assimilating into his style". It is familiar to music lovers the world over and the sure instinct of the public has never allowed it to slip from view.

Grieg and the Norwegian pianist Edmund Neupert who gave the first performance of the Piano Concerto in Copenhagen in 1869.

Chapter 7

A Letter from Liszt

Although Grieg longed to escape the drudgery of teaching and his life in Christiania, his petitions for scholarships to travel and study abroad were consistently turned down. Already after his debut concert in Bergen he had applied for one but to no avail. But with the success of the Piano Concerto behind him, he was determined to make another attempt. He was heartened by public support from Bjørnson in a newspaper article. However the decisive factor that carried most weight with the authorities was yet to come.

While he had been in Rome, Grieg had met the Danish pianist, Niels Ravnkilde. They were to become lifelong friends and corresponded right up until Ravnkilde's death in 1890. He was 20 years older than Grieg, and had settled in Rome where he taught the piano privately. He was chairman of the Scandinavian Society, where Grieg had met both Liszt and Ibsen. Through him he learned that Liszt had spoken favourably of his music. Knowing of Liszt's kindness towards young artists, which was prodigious, he asked Ravnkilde whether he would approach Liszt on his behalf for a testimonial or letter of support. Grieg did not really expect anything much would come of it, and had almost forgotten the matter when a couple of months later, a letter came that lifted his spirits from the despair into which Christiania and the Norwegian winter had plunged him.

Franz Liszt at about the time of his letter to Grieg (photograph by Reutlinger in the Mansell collection.

"Monsieur, it gives me great pleasure to tell you of the sincere enjoyment I derived from a perusal of your sonata (opus 8).

It bears witness to a strong talent for composition, a talent that is reflective, inventive, provided with excellent material, and which needs only to follow its natural inclinations to rise to a high rank. I comfort myself with the belief that you will find in your country the success and encouragement you deserve; nor will you miss them elsewhere; and if you visit Germany this winter I invite you cordially to spend some time at Weimar, that we may become acquainted.

Receive, monsieur, the assurance of my deepest regard.

Franz Liszt,

(29 December 1868, Rome)

This letter along with the triumphant reception of the Piano Concerto was decisive in tipping the scales in his favour and securing him his longed-for travelling scholarship. Even so the authorities at the Ministry of Education still kept the young composer on tenterhooks for six months before giving him the good news. And longer was to elapse before he could embark on his pilgrimage to the south.

Something dreadful had happened a little earlier in the summer of 1868 that drove everything else from his mind. Infant mortality was high in nineteenth-century Europe, just as it is in third world countries now. On 21 May, only a few days after they had arrived in the family home, Landås, and barely a month after her first birthday, Grieg's daughter contracted a fever and died from inflammation of the brain. Her loss

Liszt's letter to Grieg.

Monsieur,

Il m'est fort agréable de vous dire le sincère plaisir que m'a causé la lecture de votre Sonate (Oeuvre 8). Elle témoigne d'un talent de composition vigoureux, réfléchi, inventif, d'excellente étoffe, — lequel n'a qu'à suivre sa voie naturelle pour monter à un haut rang. Je me plais à croire que vous trouvez dans votre pays les succès et encouragements que vous méritez; ils ne vous manqueront pas ailleurs non plus; et si vous venez en Allemagne cet hiver, je vous invite cordialement à vous arrêter un peu à Weimar, pour que nous fassions tout à fait bonne connaissance.

Veuillez bien recevoir, Monsieur, l'assurance de mes sentiments d'estime et considération très distingués.

F. Liszt

29 Décembre 68

Rome

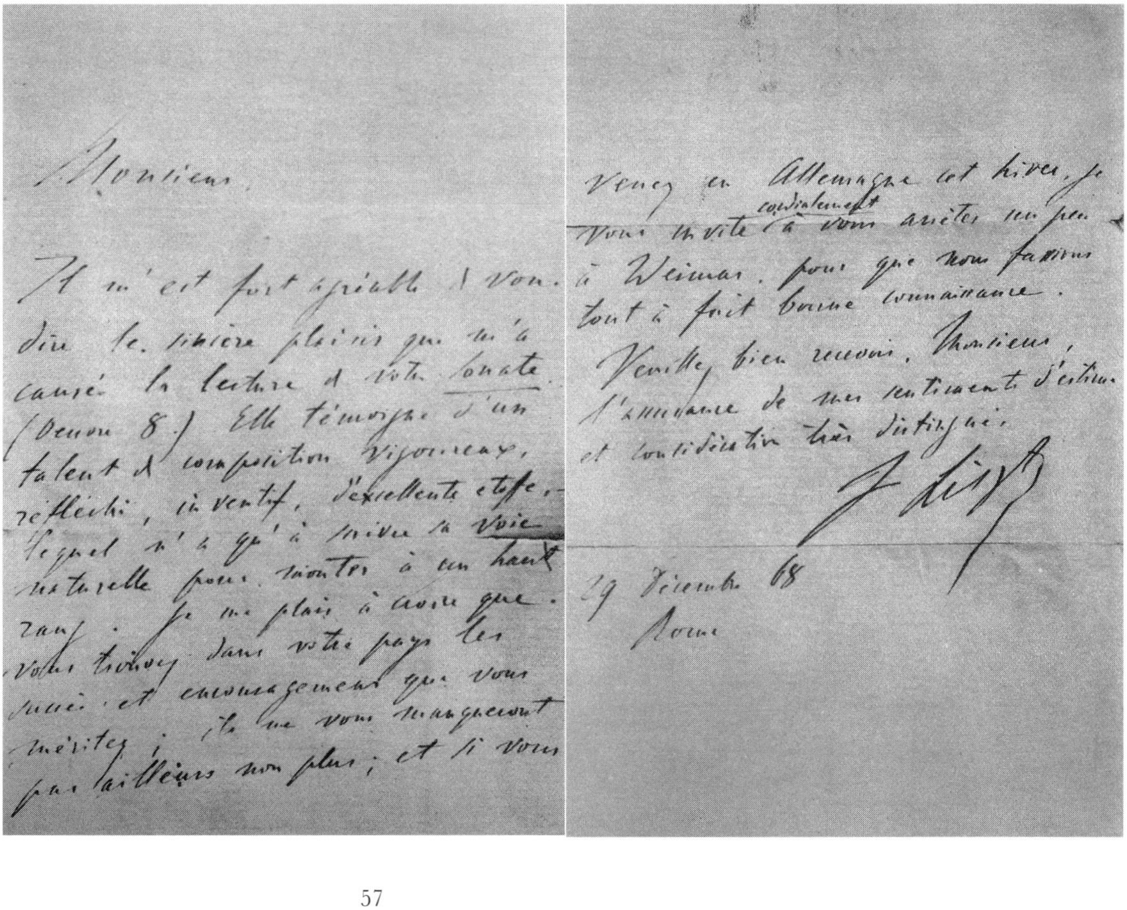

naturally overshadowed all else that summer. Grieg and Nina's world was shattered, though by way of escape, Edvard threw himself into his work. But although he "worked through" his grief, he felt the loss deeply and until quite late in life. There is a poignant reference later in life to the anguish he felt, in a letter to his Dutch friend, the violinist and composer, Julius Röntgen, who suffered a similar fate. Grieg spent these desolate weeks poring over Lindeman's *Norwegian Mountain Melodies* which were to influence him all his life from the G minor Ballade, op. 24, through to his very last work, the *Four Psalms*, op. 74.

Grieg had the power to create in a few brushstrokes a mood picture that is strong in atmosphere and that resonates equally powerfully in the memory. His songs immediately proclaim their strong artistic identity, and a total absorption of Norway's rich folk resource into his bloodstream. One of the songs inspired by the events of this summer, is *Millom rosor (Among roses)*, though it did not appear in print until many years later, when Grieg included it in *Romancer Ældre og Nyare (Songs Old and New)*, op. 39. The poet, Kristofer Janson had suffered a similar loss of a child so his poem struck a sympathetic chord. The first stanza pictures a mother playing with her son in the garden; the second tells of her bereavement and finds her praying that she may always see him resting among a bed of roses. These painful months in 1869 saw him finish a set of *Romancer og Sange (Nine Songs)*, op. 18, which include five settings of Hans Christian Andersen, which were published later the same year. But the main work of the summer was the set of *25 Norske Folkeviser og Danser (25 Norwegian Folk-songs and Dances)*, op.17, based on Lindeman's collection.

Hans Andersen,
the Danish poet.

Chapter 8

With Liszt in Rome

Liszt's generous encouragement of young musicians was legendary – and not only the young! There was a hardly a musician in Europe who could not testify to his many kindnesses. His long years of concert touring were over, and the larger part of his creative life was behind him. The 1850s had been his most fertile period when he had written the *Faust Symphony* and so many of the tone poems, and as musical director of the Court at Weimar, had introduced among other things Wagner's *Tannhäuser* and *Lohengrin* and much else

Piazza Narona in the 1870s.

The opening page of the Violin Sonata No. 2 in G major, op. 13 in Grieg's hand.

besides. In the 1860s his daughter Cosima had left her husband to elope with Wagner. By the time Grieg visited him, Liszt was in his late fifties and enjoying a perambulatory existence, spending the summer months in Weimar, the winter and spring in his native Hungary, and the remainder of his time in Rome where he received the young Norwegian. He had already taken holy orders in 1865, becoming the Abbé Liszt.

Grieg and Nina set out on their journey in September 1869 but spent a couple of months in Copenhagen, where he gave two concerts. In one he conducted the piano concerto with Neupert playing the solo part. Then the Griegs packed their bags and went to Germany, stopping in Berlin, Leipzig and

Vienna where they lingered for ten days. Then, they went on to Rome via Venice and Florence, arriving there in time for Christmas. Grieg left a vivid picture of his four-month stay in Italy; his visit to Amalfi, Naples and Paestum, and above all his two-day encounter with Liszt. His letters home convey something of the excitement that he felt when he presented himself with a package containing his most recent violin sonata, No. 2 in G major, op. 13. These letters bring the occasion graphically to life.

"[Liszt's] eyes fastened with a hungry expression on the package I had under my arm... And his long spider-like fingers approached the package in such an alarming manner that I thought it advisable to open it at once. He now commenced to turn over the pages, that is to say, he skimmed over the first movement of the sonata, and that there was no sham about his really reading it, he soon showed by significant nods or a 'bravo,' or a *'sehr schön'* (beautiful) when he came across one of the best passages. He had now become interested, but my courage dropped below zero when he asked me to play the sonata. It had never occurred to me to attempt the whole score on the piano, and I was anxious, on the other hand, to avoid stumbling when playing for him. But there was no helping it.

So I started on his splendid American grand piano, a Chickering. Right at the beginning, where the violin starts in with a rather baroque but national passage, he exclaimed: *'Ei wie keck! Nun hören Sie mal, das gefällt mir. Noch einmal bitte!'* ('How bold that is! Look here, I like that. Once more, please!') And where the violin again comes in adagio, he played the violin part on the upper octaves of the piano with an expression so beautiful, so marvellously true and singing, that it made me smile inwardly. These were the first tones I heard Liszt play; and now we passed rapidly into the *Allegro*, he taking the violin part, and I the piano. My spirits rose gradually, because his approval, which he manifested in a truly lavish way, did me good, and I felt myself imbued with the strongest feelings of gratitude. When we had come to the end of the first movement, I asked his permission to play a piano solo, selecting the minuet from the set of *Humoresques*. When I had played the first eight bars and repeated them, he sang along the melody, and did it with an expression of a certain heroic power which I understood very well. I observed that it was the national peculiarities he liked; this I had suspected before going to him, and had therefore taken with me the pieces in which I had tried to strike the national strings.

After playing the minuet I felt that if it were possible to get Liszt to play for me, now was the time; he was visibly inspired. I asked him, and he shrugged his shoulders a little; but when I said it could not be his intention that I should leave the south without having heard a single note by him, he made a turn and then muttered: '*Nun ich spiele was Sie wollen, ich bin nicht so!*' ('Very well, I'll play whatever you like, I am not like that!'); and he straight away seized a score he had lately finished, a kind of funeral procession to the grave of Tasso, a supplement to his famous symphonic poem for orchestra, *Tasso: Lamento e Trionfo*. Then he sat down and put the keys in motion. Yes, I assure you, he spewed out, if I may use so inelegant an expression, one volley after another of heat and flame and vivid thoughts. It sounded as if he had evoked the flames of Tasso. He made the colours glaring, but such a subject is just the thing for him; the expression of tragic grandeur is his strong point. I did not know what to admire most in him, the composer or the pianist, for he played superbly. No, he does not really play – one forgets he is a musician, he becomes a prophet."

Grieg evidently had no idea of the faux-pas he had made in even asking Liszt to play. His most intimate friends, even the Princess Sayn-Wittgenstein, never dared to. It says much for the charm Grieg must have exercised that Liszt chose to make an exception to his rule on this occasion.

"When this was done Liszt said cheerfully, 'Now let us go on with the sonata,' to which I naturally retorted: 'No, thank you, after this I couldn't.' But now comes the best part of the story. Liszt exclaimed, '*Nun, warum nicht, geben Sie mal her, dann werde ich es thun.*' ('Why not? Then give it me, I'll do it.') Now you must bear in mind, in the first place, that he had never seen or heard the sonata, and in the second place that it was a sonata with a violin part, now above, now below, independent of the pianoforte part. And what does Liszt do? He plays the whole thing, root and branch, violin and piano, nay, more, for he played fuller, more broadly. The violin got its due right in the middle of the piano part. He was literally over the whole piano at once, without missing a note, and how he did play! With grandeur, beauty, genius, unique comprehension."

To another correspondent Grieg wrote, "As an un-heard of favour I was asked to visit him, and he proceeded to play – I tell you, I don't care if I ever hear anyone else play the piano. The point is that this is not piano playing. One forgets the pianist, the instrument, and all that nonsense; one is alone with a giant who marshals a legion of spirits in headlong flight with all of his unbridled fancy."

Liszt's phenomenal powers as a sight-reader were legendary, and having already witnessed his prowess in the violin sonata, Grieg was naturally curious to see whether he would really sight-read the concerto. "Personally, I considered it impossible," he wrote home. "But Liszt on the other hand was of an entirely different opinion. He said to me, 'Would you like to play it?' I hastened to say that I couldn't! Liszt then took the manuscript, went to the piano and, with a smile peculiar to himself, said to all those who were present: 'Well, now I'll show you that I can't either'. Then he began. And in view of what he subsequently accomplished, I must say that it would be impossible to imagine anything more sublime. He played the first part rather rapidly, and the result was that the opening sounded rather slapdash, but later on, when I had an opportunity to indicate the tempo, he played as he alone and no one else can. It is significant that he played the cadenza, which is among the technically most difficult parts of the concerto, perfectly... He doesn't just play; no, he converses and comments at the same time. He carries on a brilliant conversation not with one person but with the entire audience, distributing significant nods to right and left mainly when he is particularly pleased with something. In the *Adagio* and to an even greater extent in the *Finale*, he reached a peak both in execution and in the praise he gave... Time and again when disappointments and bitterness come I shall think of his words, and the memory of this hour will have a wonderful power to sustain me in days of adversity."

Undoubtedly it was the national element that appealed to Liszt. When the G sharp at the very end of the concerto is contradicted by a G, Liszt exclaimed "Splendid! That's the real thing. I heard something of the kind the other day from Smetana. Keep on, I tell you. You've got what it takes, and don't let them frighten you!" With these words ringing in his ears, he started on the journey back to Copenhagen where he and Nina remained for a couple of months before returning to spend the summer in Bergen. He would have many occasions to recall Liszt's support and encouragement in the coming years.

Chapter 9

Operatic Plans with Bjørnson

Considering the fact that Scandinavia boasts so many great singers from Jenny Lind and Christina Nilsson in the last century down to Flagstad, Jussi Björling, Melchior and Birgit Nilsson in our own, it is surprising that it has produced no great operas. For all their excellence Nielsen's *Saul and David* and *Maskarade* have never conquered the international stage. Yet all

Grieg in 1872.

64

the major Nordic composers have been drawn towards the genre at one time or another. The nearest that Grieg ever came to opera was *Olav Trygvason*, to a libretto by Bjørnstjerne Bjørnson. The latter's failure to provide it put their collaboration and indeed their friendship under great strain.

Grieg had met Bjørnson in the summer of 1866 and the two had taken to each other. Bjørnson was an outsize and colourful personality who spoke his mind openly; he was not conventional and was a fervent nationalist. Eleven years older than Grieg, he had already established himself as a leading poet and dramatist, second only in importance to Ibsen. Although his plays have not held the stage outside Norway, his influence at the time was enormous and his position unassailable. His first novel deals with the fate of ordinary country people and was written in everyday language, both of which were unusual in

Bjørnstjerne Bjørnson, the Norwegian dramatist, poet and polemicist.

Norway at the time. In addition he wrote short stories and plays with a modern, realistic streak and was a formidable poet. (Among the poems, as we have seen, are the stanzas that his cousin Nordraak set, which were to become the Norwegian national anthem.) Although it is difficult to believe nowadays, Bjørnson was regarded in his lifetime as almost the equal of Ibsen, and he had a strong following in Europe, particularly France. He was active not only in the campaign against the union with Sweden, but in all sorts of social and political questions, the Peace Movement, the oppression of minority peoples such as the Slovaks, where the publicity he gave to their persecution is still remembered. He expended tremendous energy on correspondence and newspaper articles, and his polemical activities took its toll on his creative energy in later life. Unlike Ibsen and Grieg, his reputation outside Norway faded steeply after his death.

Bjørnson spent much of his time abroad – in Paris, Rome, Schwatz in the Tyrol and in Copenhagen – but in October 1868, he was back in Christiania. "Bjørnson is here," Grieg wrote to Ravnkilde – "and where he is, there are also vitality and imagination." Grieg had soon become disenchanted with life in Christiania. A small town with fewer than 100,000 inhabitants, most of them narrow-minded and conformist. Against this background Bjørnson stood out, and made an ever stronger impression. In Grieg's own words, "he shaped my personality in many ways... he made me a democrat, artistically and politically. As he later put it in a letter to Iver Holter, "He gave me the courage to follow my own instincts. This period was a marvellous time with its abundance of courage and faith!"

In such a provincial climate music hardly flourished. It is difficult to imagine from our vantage point how few were the opportunities to hear music unless one made it oneself. As Grieg told his American biographer Henry Finck, "The public's attitude at that time was so primitive, and their understanding of artistic interpretation was far too barbarous for them to be able to appreciate performances that gave major emphasis to the life of the spirit. It got to the point where we only made music at home or among our own circle of friends." There was no permanent orchestra at this time in Christiania. Nor was the situation much better in Stockholm, apart from the Opera, nor in Helsinki which had to wait until 1882 before Robert Kajanus put its orchestra on a permanent footing. As we have seen, Copenhagen with its more vigorous artistic and musical life was a different matter.

Where Bjørnson was, there also was this "vitality and imagination". In the early 1870s he was the predominant source of inspiration for the composer. The *Four Songs*, op. 21, the setting of *Fra Monte Pincio (From Monte Pincio)* and *Prinsessen (The Princess)*, are all Bjørnson settings and are among Grieg's finest songs. Apart from these, there were Bjørnson settings on a larger scale such as the cantata, *Føran Sydens Kloster (Before a Southern Convent)*, op. 20, and the melodrama, *Bergliot*, op. 42. Despite their widely differing opus numbers for which there is a good explanation, both come from 1871. *Before a Southern Convent* is a rarity nowadays, seldom heard even in the Nordic countries, and until recently, even difficult to find on records. Its text comes from Bjørnson's dramatic poem, *Arnljot Gelline*. At one time Grieg even toyed with the idea of basing an opera on it. The episode Grieg chose from the poem, tells how Ingigerd, the daughter of a chief from Jämtland, has seen her father murdered by the bandit, Arnljot. He was on the point of raping her but spared her out of pity. Despite his crimes, Ingigerd (the second 'g' is pronounced as a 'y' as in yes) feels a strange attraction for him, and in expiation for her guilt at these sentiments, takes refuge abroad and presents herself at the portals of a convent in a foreign land. Here she is questioned about her reasons for wanting to embrace a cloistered life, and finally admitted to the order. The piece is for soprano and contralto soloists, a female choir and orchestra. It is not what one might call top-drawer Grieg and the final choir of the nuns is relatively conventional. However, Bjørnson thought it wonderful and Grieg himself was sufficiently pleased with it to consider dedicating it to one of his great heros, the Danish composer, Hartmann. Doubtless he would have done, had he not discovered that Hartmann himself had set the same text. His high opinion of it persisted and he felt sufficiently confident of its merits to dedicate it to Liszt. And when he conducted it in Germany a few years later with Nina as the soprano soloist, it scored a great success.

Bjørnson had been so enthusiastic about *Before a Southern Convent* that Grieg was encouraged to embark on a melodrama, *Bergliot*. Melodrama, the reciting of a poetic text to a musical accompaniment, has fallen out of fashion in our day but enjoyed much popularity in the eighteenth and nineteenth centuries. In *Bergliot*, Bjørnson turned to the *Heimskringla Sagas*, the same source as he had done for *Sigurd the Crusader (Sigurd Jorsalfar)*, for which Grieg was to provide music the following year. Grieg's melodrama for speaker and orchestra begins at the point where Bergliot's husband, Einar Tambarskjelve and their son, Eindride, had been lured to a meeting where they are brutally murdered by King Harald Hårdråde. Bergliot upbraids her kinsmen for their cowardice in not avenging them and invokes the retribution of the gods. Grieg's aim was to compose a colourful orchestral piece with spoken narration, but he had to content himself with speaker and piano. There was no possibility of mounting a performance with orchestra at the time, and so Grieg put it to one side. He returned to the score and orchestrated it during the autumn of 1885, hence its much later opus number.

Bergliot was a great success at its première in Christiania in 1885 – indeed, strange though it may seem, it also enjoyed something of a vogue in France, albeit a brief one. Nordic mythology was all the rage in the late 1880s and France, like England, also experienced a vogue for Ibsen. John Horton argues that the harmonic language of *Bergliot* may well have had its influence on French impressionism and points to the anticipation of *Danseuses de Delphes* from the First Book of Debussy's *Préludes* at one point during its course.

Then, in this great sequence of Bjørnson pieces, comes *Landkjenning* (*Landsighting*), which is related in its subject-matter but not in a musical way to the opera that they were soon to plan, and the incidental music to *Sigurd Jorsalfar* (*Sigurd the Crusader*). Both were ready by the spring of 1872. The music for *Sigurd Jorsalfar* was written early in the year at high speed so as to be ready for its première on 10 April, and both were performed in Christiania on Norwegian Constitution Day (17 May) with Grieg himself conducting. At this stage there were eight movements in all, six of them instrumental and two vocal. Since the leading actor, Hjalmar Hammar was not well endowed vocally and was required to sing 'The King's Song' at the end of the play, the performance was not without its problems. Bjørnson had fallen out with the theatre management and refused to have anything to do with the production. But he was persuaded to attend the May performance and thought the First Act "really rough". However despite all this, the play was received by a storm of applause and remained in repertory for some time. Grieg made a concert arrangement of this music in 1892, when among other things he expanded and re-scored the *Homage March*.

Landsighting tells of the return of Olav Trygvason to Norway over a thousand years ago in 995, and his plans to build a church in Nidaros (Trondheim). The first performance of the piece took place at a function to raise funds for the restoration of the church. On that occasion it was scored for baritone, two male-voice choirs, wind ensemble and organ but subsequently, in 1881, Grieg reworked it for baritone, one male voice choir, orchestra and organ. Its success, as well as that of *Sigurd Jorsalfar*, prompted Bjørnson to look towards a more ambitious dramatic project to interest Grieg. And so, the idea of an opera on Olav Trygvason, the tenth-century king who converted Norway to Christianity, was born.

In the middle of 1873 Bjørnson sent Grieg the first three scenes, which so fired the composer's enthusiasm that he had drafted a setting in short score by the middle of the summer. Grieg then wrote asking for more text but when Bjørnson visited Grieg at Landås in August, he brought nothing. He was just about to return to Italy where he was living, but lost no time in emphasizing the importance of their collaborating closely on the next stages of the work. He pressed the composer to join him in the Mediterranean but Grieg was simply not able to leave Norway. He still had burdensome commitments in Christiania which paid his bills – just about – and it was not until 1874 that a government stipend enabled him to cut himself free for composition. Bjørnson had been instrumental in securing this stipend, so his feelings can be imagined when he learnt that Grieg's thoughts were turning in a totally different direction – namely, the score to Ibsen's *Peer Gynt*. He was not best pleased. Their relations abruptly cooled and fell to somewhere near zero. Yet it was Bjørnson who was to blame for the fact that Grieg's operatic plans never reached fruition, for however often he was pressed, he consistently failed to deliver a libretto.

As Grieg put it in a letter to Niels Ravnkilde, "Bjørnson, as he may have told you, has promised me a text for a Norwegian music drama, which I have already done a little work on. But unfortunately I have other obligations that I must take care of first before I can do any more with this project; and besides Bjørnson refuses to give me any more text unless I am near him – a harsh demand but one I wish I could accede to, because I really am very fond of him. Give him my greetings and tell him that I wait longingly for a letter from him, and that I will wait as long as I must, albeit not as long as Solveig in *Peer Gynt*: for a lifetime" (9 January 1875).

The three scenes or tableaux Grieg had composed in 1873 are all that remain of the opera. In musical character they are closer to a cantata. The setting of the First Scene is a pagan temple near Trondheim, where an anxious throng awaits the arrival of "the evil Olav", herald of the new faith. After an orchestral introduction, two soloists, a high priest and a woman, alternate with chorus in their appeals to the ancient Norse gods for help. In the Second Scene a priestess appears. She utters sinister incantations and chants magic formulae, casting runic characters into the holy fire. The scene ends with the high priest lifting "great father Odin's" horn and the chorus announcing that sacred dances are to be held in honour of Odin. The Third Scene is devoted to wild dances such as a circle dance and an intense sword dance with constantly changing formations.

To step out of a strict chronological framework for a moment, it was 15 years before Grieg's thoughts returned to *Olav Trygvason*. He decided to revise and orchestrate the three scenes for a concert in Christiania which he was to conduct in October 1889. He also took the opportunity to offer an olive branch to the poet in the form of its dedication, "and in so doing I offer you proof that ever since we parted I have continued to love you and all that you stand for – and express a fervent hope that this work, which was the cause of our losing contact with each other, might also be the thing that brings us together again!" Bjørnson's response was equally generous in spirit and a reconciliation was effected. But by this time the poet had completely lost interest in the idea, and Grieg himself had gone off the boil, so that the opera remained a chimera.

Two years later the scenes from *Olav Trygvason* came to London and among the audience was the playwright, George Bernard Shaw who was then writing music criticism that remains peerless in terms of wit and sparkle. "The world has suffered many things through Grieg's experiments in the grand style of composition; but assuredly the climax was reached on Saturday week, when his setting of three scenes from Bjørnsons's *Olav Trygvason* was performed at the Crystal Palace. I have no idea of the age at which Grieg perpetrated this tissue of puerilities but if he was a day over eighteen the exploit is beyond excuse" (1 April 1891). It goes without saying that Shaw was, of course, fully aware that far from being a youthful work, the three scenes had been composed when Grieg was 30 and revised in 1888 and published only the year before.

Despite Shaw's entertaining dismissal of the piece, Benestad and Schjelderup-Ebbe come closer to the truth in their study of the composer. True, there are no arias or big set-pieces. Grieg adopts a declamatory style sometimes reminiscent of Wagner, particularly, I would say, in the Second Scene, though it remains in essence very much Grieg's own. "What gives *Olav Trygvason* a certain nobility", they say, "is the composer's imaginative use of the orchestra. Grieg produces

Grieg and Svendsen photographed
together. It throws into relief
Grieg's diminutive height!

passages that are sometimes coarse and full of contrast, creating tonal colours that cause the dark contours of the work to stand out sharply."

If his relationship with Bjørnson formed one of the twin pillars in his artistic life, his collaboration with Johan Svendsen was the other. In 1871 Grieg founded the *Musikforeningen* (Music Association), a continuation of the Philharmonic Society which had disbanded in 1868, and on his return to Norway in the autumn of 1872, Svendsen joined him. Building an audience for orchestral concerts was an uphill struggle but Grieg introduced a lot of music new to the public. His first concert included Gade's *Elverskud (The Fairy Spell)*, in which Nina was one of the soloists, and Beethoven's Second Symphony. At the same concert he also conducted the Prelude to *Sigurd Slembe*, Svendsen's most recent work. Another important work was the Mozart *Requiem*.

Until Svendsen's return Grieg felt that he was carrying the main burden alone. And the fact is that after Halfdan Kjerulf's death in 1868 he was. He told Aimar Grønvold in the 1880s, he could only look back on those years "with bitterness at the indifference – yes, the contempt and disdain that were shown for Norwegian music". Strong words no doubt, but ones which were hardly misplaced. Even the Christiania première of the Piano Concerto had been badly attended. With Svendsen's homecoming, he felt the first signs of change.

During the next few seasons Grieg and Svendsen presented a varied and interesting repertoire. Svendsen conducted the première of his newly composed *Carnival in Paris* on 26 October 1872 and in the following season Grieg presented Schumann's *Paradise and the Peri*. Among his chorus was a young law student, also a native of Bergen, who asked Grieg if he would give him piano lessons. It would not be long before he became one of his firmest and most loyal friends. His name was Frants Beyer and he was later Grieg's neighbour at Næsset (the word means promontory) opposite Troldhaugen outside Bergen. As well as running his law practice, he was an accomplished musician, and became a close confidant. Without their lifelong correspondence our picture of the composer would be far less complete.

Chapter 10

Peer Gynt

Although Grieg and Ibsen had met in Rome in 1866, they had never become close. Nor were they ever to become so. Yet it was obvious to the great dramatist that Grieg was a composer of outstanding gifts and strong personality. Moreover it was obvious from the comments he had made about Ibsen's play, *Brand* that Grieg had a real understanding of the playwright. In 1874 Ibsen had decided to turn his dramatic poem, *Peer Gynt* which was by this time going into its third printing, into a work

Grieg at the time
of Peer Gynt.

for the stage. So it was to Grieg that his thoughts turned when the idea of extensive incidental music first surfaced in his mind. He wrote to Grieg from Dresden on 23 January and his letter went into great detail as to where the music was to come in the drama. Indeed he could scarcely have been more specific in his directions.

Despite his commitments to Bjørnson, Grieg did not hesitate for a moment. As well as being positive his response must have been immediate since Ibsen wrote again on 8 February, "How much music and for which scenes you will compose it, I naturally leave entirely to you; in this matter a composer obviously must have a completely free hand... I will probably visit Norway this summer, and then I could perhaps have the pleasure of discussing this project with you – and also of reviving our common memories of Rome."

Ibsen specified his plans in great detail. The First Act was to remain virtually intact with "a few cuts in the dialogue". He then goes on, "With the help of ballet, much more must be made of the wedding scene... For this a special dance melody must be composed, which can then continue to be played softly until the end of the act. In the Second Act the scene with the herd girls may be handled musically in whatever way you think fit but there must be devilry in it. The monologue I have thought of as being handled melodramatically with chords played in the background. The same goes for the scene with Peer and the Woman in Green. Some kind of musical accompaniment must also be created for the scene in the hall of the Mountain King though the speeches in this section are to be considerably shortened. The scene with the Great Bøyg, which is to be given in full, must also have a musical accompaniment; bird calls must be sung, and church bells and hymns must be heard in the distance." The Great Bøyg is a mysterious character whose voice personifies Peer's conscience.

He goes on to ask for a soft accompaniment for the scene depicting the death of Aase but then details his plan for the Fourth Act. "Nearly the whole of the Fourth Act is to be omitted. In its place I have imagined a large-scale tone poem suggesting Peer Gynt's wandering throughout the world; American, English and French melodies might be interwoven, growing and fading one by one." Ibsen's letter held out the prospect of productions in both Copenhagen and Stockholm, and suggested that the performance rights should be shared between them.

It soon became obvious to Grieg that he had taken on a mammoth task. Once he was able to leave Christiania for

The composing hut where Grieg worked on *Peer Gynt*.

Bergen in the summer, he settled down to work in earnest. His circumstances had been considerably eased by the award of the state stipend earlier in the year. Work on *Peer Gynt* was proceeding slowly and there was no chance of his completing it by the autumn. "With the exception of a few places it is a terribly difficult play for which to write music," he told Frants Beyer in a letter of 27 August 1874, one of the few places being the scene in which Solveig sings. This was among the first that he completed. "I have also written something for the scene in the hall of the Mountain King – something that I literally can't bear listening to because it absolutely reeks of cow-dung, exaggerated Norwegian nationalism, and trollish self-satisfaction! But I have a hunch that the irony will be discernible."

Ibsen had entrusted the play to Ludvig Josephson, the director of the Christiania Theatre, and a producer of the realistic-romantic school. His much-admired staging of Meyerbeer's *L'Africaine* at the Royal Opera, Stockholm only a few years before in 1867 had been such a resounding triumph. Not only did he enjoy Ibsen's confidence but he was also a realist in not hurrying Grieg. In the autumn he reassured him that the production would not be mounted until January at the earliest. In the event it was to be another year before *Peer Gynt* was first staged and Grieg continued working on the score in Denmark where he spent the rest of the autumn. In early January 1875 he wrote to Bjørnson in Italy, "it has gone as you predicted: it hangs over me like a nightmare, and I can't possibly get it out of the way until the spring". But, he added "the performance of *Peer Gynt* just now can do some good in Christiania, where materialism is trying to rise up and stifle everything that we regard as lofty and holy. There is a need for one more mirror, I think, in which all the egotism can be seen, and such a mirror is *Peer Gynt*; then you will come home and rebuild. For it cannot be denied: the people must see their own ugliness before you can do any good, but once their eyes are opened you are just the man to lead the parade".

However, apart from his work on *Peer Gynt*, 1875 was to prove a difficult year for Grieg. If he did not greatly care for the philistine atmosphere of Christiania, it would seem that Christiania did not much care for him. His music was still rarely performed in the Norwegian capital. Over the next few years his links with Christiania were to grow looser, and he spent less and less time there. In 1875 this was dictated more by circumstances than inclination, for his father's health was declining and he spent the remainder of it in Bergen close to the family. In fact this was to prove a traumatic year for him, for during the autumn he suffered the loss not only of his father but his mother too. He retreated into himself and apart from giving a handful of lessons, led a reclusive existence. Much of his grief was poured into the Ballade in G minor op. 24, a set of variations on an old Norwegian folk song. Poignant and deeply felt, the Ballade must be numbered among his greatest works. Such was the emotion it aroused and the pain which accompanied its composition that Grieg could hardly bear to play it in later life.

When *Peer Gynt* was eventually staged for the first time on 24 February 1876, it enjoyed unprecedented success. It lasted over five hours and the audience was obviously in no doubt as to its importance and quality. It was what would have been called a "smash hit", had it been New York and not Christiania, and it was given 36 performances during the succeeding weeks. One thing is abundantly clear. Although a good part of the credit for its success was the acting of Henrik Klausen as Peer, an even greater part was the music of Edvard Grieg. Ibsen was not in the audience. Nor was Grieg, who did not want to face the world so soon after the death of his parents. Perhaps that was just as well, because at the première, one of the Norwegian dailies, *Morgenbladet* reported, "the music is certainly in its totality a most exceptional piece of work – insofar as one dares to judge after this single performance, when many in the audience displayed such a lack of appropriate interest and respect for the composer that they carried on noisy conversations during many of the numbers". And there were many numbers in which to converse – 26 in fact!

Grieg's absence from Christiania at this time proved a blessing in disguise for posterity, for it compelled him to convey his wishes by letter. Hence we can see exactly what his intentions were for each of the numbers. He did not see a performance until November and it is clear also that he had been in no hurry to do so. Already the previous year he had been apprehensive of the quality of the orchestra – and had written to Bjørnson on 21 February 1875, "Yesterday I heard how things stand with respect to music at the Christiania Theatre, as a result of which I am today writing to both Ibsen and Josephson that I consider it my duty not to deliver anything... so long as the orchestra is not at adequate strength. It is absolutely scandalous, the worst that it has ever been, and Svendsen says that if the situation continues we will in the course of a few years have no orchestra at all in Norway's capital city."

Ibsen was fully supportive in urging him to make no concessions. "Score your music according to an ideal standard and let them worry about how to perform it. Anything less than that would be unworthy of a man such as you, and moreover would harm us both." After the première and before he had seen it, Grieg wrote on similar lines to his friend and contemporary, Johan Peter Selmer, "One can take satisfaction in acclaim when one has a good conscience in relation to one's own artistic ideals; but that does not apply to me and that wretched *Peer Gynt* music, for every moment I had to banish my ideals in order to cover up for a poor orchestra and enhance the popular stage effects. If I had had the strength to be my better self, it goes without saying that I would have been there to see to it that my intentions were realized; but you can surely

Henrik Ibsen in the mid-1870s.

understand that under these circumstances I preferred to be elsewhere." For some years after this, he resisted requests for the score and parts insisting that the music was to be heard only in a theatrical context. Indeed as late as 1882, he wrote to the conductor Johan Hennum, who had conducted the original production, that the "instrumentation didn't please me then, and it does so even less now".

Theatrical history may have been made by the Christiania performance for never had so ambitious an enterprise been undertaken in Norway but it was struck by disaster less than a year after the first night when the sets and costumes were destroyed by fire. Over 15 years were to elapse before *Peer Gynt* was staged again there and it was only then, in 1892, that Ibsen saw it for the first time. As with the Piano Concerto, Grieg felt that he could never quite escape from *Peer Gynt* and although piano arrangements of some of the most popular pieces, such as 'Solveig's Song' and 'Anitra's Dance' were published only a month or so after *Peer Gynt* had opened, albeit from a

Copenhagen publisher, Grieg maintained his ban on its use in the concert hall.

When *Peer Gynt* returned to the stage again, it was almost ten years later in 1885, in a lavish Copenhagen production with Henrik Klausen again in the title rôle. This gave Grieg the opportunity he needed of overhauling all the music, and refurbishing it so that "it could present itself decently clothed". In the intervening years Grieg had learnt a great deal more about the orchestra and had become a proficient conductor. On this occasion Grieg felt sufficiently confident to involve himself with the production and described the turmoil. "In the café I am bombarded by copyists and music directors who grab the pages from me one at a time as soon as I am finished with them. Two pieces gave me much satisfaction at the first rehearsal. They were the introduction to the Second Act and the scene with the herd girls. The latter you wouldn't even recognise. When I first conceived it I felt something, but now I know something: that is the difference. It has acquired life, colour and devilry – which were really not there before because the instrumentation was so defective." Great trouble was taken over the production for which some new numbers were added. He enlisted the help of two Danish colleagues to score the 'Bridal Procession' from the second of the three *Pictures from Folk Life*, op. 19 written in the early 1870s, which was inserted before the wedding scene in the First Act, and three of the *Norwegian Dances*, op. 35 which were pressed into service for the scene in the Hall of the Mountain King. To judge by his letters of January 1886 to Frants Beyer (reproduced by Benestad and Schjelderup-Ebbe) he would seem to have enjoyed himself thoroughly even if it was hard work.

But Grieg was not yet finished with *Peer*. Not only was the clamour for concert suites unabated but every new production brought demands for additional material. In 1892 Bjørnson's son, Bjørn who was by this time director of the Christiania Theatre (and had incidentally married Ibsen's daughter) embarked on a particularly bold course. Not only did he design the sets and direct the production but he also played the title rôle. He asked for more music for the scene with the Bøyg and for some new material for other scenes.

Grieg had, however, been sufficiently pleased with the revision he had made for Copenhagen in 1885 to consider at last making the orchestral suites for which there was such evident demand. The First, op. 46, comprising 'Morning Mood', 'The Death of Aase', 'Anitra's Dance' and 'In the Hall of the Mountain King', was put into its definitive form in 1887-88.

Bjørnson's son, Bjørn as Peer Gynt in the 1892 Christiania production.

The Second, op. 55, also included 'The Abduction of the Bride and Ingrid's Lament' from the First Act of the play, and the 'Arabian Dance' from the Fourth; 'Peer Gynt's Homecoming' and 'Solveig's Song' followed a couple of years later in 1890-92. Oddly enough Grieg had originally thought to omit the 'Arabian Dance' in favour of the 'Dance of the Mountain King's Daughter' but decided against it. He also, regrettably perhaps, decided against including 'Peer Gynt's Serenade', one of the most haunting and appealing pieces in the whole score, and 'Solveig's Cradle Song'. These suites became popular all over the world during the last decade of his life and still remain so today.

Grieg still tinkered with the score for a 1901 production in Christiania, revising the orchestration of the opening prelude and the scene with Peer and the herd girls. His hopes that the complete score would be published in his lifetime were disappointed. It was not until 1908, that his younger friend and colleague, the composer Johan Halvorsen who had conducted the 1901 production, saw it into print. But his version is vulnerable on several counts. It omits numbers that Grieg had definitely included in the score, such as 'Peer Gynt and the Woman in Green' and 'The Shipwreck' and includes music that did not belong in the original, such as Halvorsen's own orchestration of 'The Bridal Procession'. It was only in 1987 that a scholarly edition by Benestad and Schjelderup-Ebbe that respects Grieg's wishes was published as Vol XVII of the Complete Edition.

Peer Gynt was not the only work of Ibsen to concern him at this time. The same year saw the *Sex Digte* (*Six Songs*), op. 25,

Johanne Dybwad as Solveig in the 1892 Christiania production.

which include *'Spillemænd'* (*'Fiddlers'*), sometimes translated as *'Minstrels'*. This song served as an important thematic element in the String Quartet in G minor a year later. Another of the Six Songs is one of his best-known, *'En svane'* (*'A swan'*). The swan is an image often found in Nordic literature as a symbol of the soul, and this is one of Ibsen's most elusive and aphoristic poems, which tells of the swan's silence until this last meeting, when with the premonition of death, it sang. The song is one of Grieg's greatest. The other set of songs of 1876 were to words of John Paulsen, with whom he was to make his pilgrimage to the first-ever Bayreuth Festival later that year.

In 1876 when Grieg had composed the first production of *Peer Gynt* he was 33, at what was to be just past the mid-point of his life. Since his childhood, life had changed in the world around him. When he had been five, the 1848 revolution had swept Europe and toppled both Metternich in Austria and Louis-Philippe in France from power. It had sown the seeds for reaction in the Habsburg empire and the emergence of Napoleon III in Paris. Mendelssohn and Chopin had died within a year of each other, and Berlioz, Wagner and Liszt were changing the face of music. By the time Grieg had reached his twenties nationalism was gathering force not only in areas subject to alien domination such as Poland or Bohemia, but foreign cultural domination was being challenged in Russia. The Italian *risorggimento* was close to fruition and the Prussian bid under Bismarck to lead a united Germany was gaining impetus. It plunged Prussia and Denmark into hostilities in 1864 and was even to engulf the two largest German-speaking nations a few years hence in 1878. Most significantly the Franco-Prussian war of 1870 was to sow the seeds of bitterness for generations to come.

By comparison Norway in its union with Sweden had relatively modest concerns. The movement for independence had still to gather genuine political momentum. It was more in the head, a distant aspiration rather than a potent political reality. Indeed Norway was self-governing to all intents and purposes, sharing with Sweden a common head of state and a joint foreign ministry. Technological progress brought the opening of a direct railway link between Christiania and Stockholm in 1871. And two years later in 1873 when Prince Oscar assumed the throne, the new king was crowned both in the Swedish capital and later in Trondheim cathedral.

It says much for the 30-year-old Grieg's eminence, at least outside Norway, that he was among the important figures in the arts and sciences to be honoured in the new reign. Both he and

Ibsen were made Knights of the the Order of St Olav. The tensions that were to grow in the 1890s and lead to the *oppløsning* (or in Swedish *upplösning*: dissolution or literally 'breaking-up' of the union) in 1905 were gently simmering below the surface but the union was not at this stage a burning issue. Grieg himself always had a strong following in Sweden and was widely played there. He had already been honoured by the Royal Swedish Academy of Music. As early as January 1873, he had given two concerts of his music, in one of which he conducted what was probably the first performance in Stockholm of the Piano Concerto with Neupart as soloist. A letter survives thanking the Swedish composer, August Söderman who had been instrumental in organising the visit. In it Grieg wrote, "you were incomparably generous and gracious towards me", and one wonders whether the subject of *Peer Gynt* which lay some twelve months in the future for Grieg had surfaced. With Söderman it lay in the past, for he had made some settings of Ibsen's dramatic poem in the late-1860s, which remained unperformed until after his death.

Chapter 11

Visit to Bayreuth

When he was in Leipzig in 1858 Grieg had fallen under the spell of Wagner's *Tannhäuser*, and it was natural that when the opportunity presented itself to go to the very first Bayreuth Festival in 1876, he should do so. He set out, armed with his scores, in the company of the poet, John Paulsen. This was the first occasion on which the *Ring* cycle was performed complete. Grieg went to cover the event for the *Bergensposten*, which published six long articles during the course of ten days. Grieg discovered to his dismay that the dress rehearsals were closed. King Ludwig II, without whose munificence not only the operas but Bayreuth itself would not have come into being, wanted to see them on his own. When Hans Richter who was conducting, had been compelled to deny Grieg admittance, he had done so in such a charming fashion that Grieg mischievously asked,

The Festspielhaus in Bayreuth.

"But what if I came in without permission?" to which he responded, "Well now, I obviously couldn't prevent something like that!" But Grieg describes it all in a very spirited and characterful fashion.

"I have received a firm promise of admission to the dress rehearsals but the matter has nonetheless become very doubtful because the King of Bavaria arrived during the night (he always travels during the night merely because he finds it romantic) and wants to have the dress rehearsal all to himself (that is because he is shy)... Well, we shall see. I am determined to attend the dress rehearsals one way or another. One does not come all the way from Norway just to stand outside" (*Bergensposten*, 6 August 1876).

Wagner bestrode the period like the collosus he is, and every composer reacted to him in some way or other. Grieg was no exception. Of course Wagnerian touches surface in *Olav Trygvason* and not only there, but for the most part, Wagner only intermittently cast his spell and Grieg never completely succumbed to it. Gerald Abraham spoke of his chromatic harmony as "an individual twig of the Wagnerian tree, a demonstration that Wagner's harmony could be employed in the charming salon piece as well as in heroic and passionate drama". But whatever qualifications Grieg might have made about Wagner, never did he at any stage fail to recognise the unique quality of Wagner's achievement. Moreover he sustained his interest and went to see both *Tristan* and *Parsifal* ten years later. A sample of his review of *Götterdämmerung* shows a refreshing enthusiasm and a complete lack of the portentous that is unusual among critics – even composer-critics.

"There is no doubt that *Götterdämmerung* is the foremost and in a dramatic sense the most effective of the four dramas. Here is enacted the great tragic conflict to which the other dramas lead up, here the fate of human beings and gods is fulfilled, here Wagner for the first time in the whole trilogy includes crowds (men and women of the Gibischungs); he knew what he was doing to keep these resources to the end. And then the rapid succession of events! And what an ending! Just as in the first drama, the Rhine maidens appear as guardians of the gold, so in the fourth they finally come into possession of it again. ... I can hardly venture to write about the music of this last gigantic work. it presents such a world of greatness and beauty that one is almost dazzled... I go home and say to myself that in

Advertisement for the first *Ring* cycle at Bayreuth from the Kölner Nachrichten, 1876.

spite of all reservations, in spite of the restlessness with which the gods are depicted, in spite of the many chromatic modulations, the ceaseless harmonic changes, which cause one to be gradually overcome by a nervous irritability and finally by complete exhaustion, despite the intricate detail, the total lack of points of repose, despite the way the whole work is poised on the extreme verge of beauty, despite everything – this music-drama is the work of a giant, the like of whom the history of art can only have seen in Michelangelo."

Though his articles are engagingly fresh, they undoubtedly

took their toll on his energies. Never robust, he did not feel up to attending a soirée at Wahnfried, Wagner's villa in Bayreuth, to which he had been invited, much to the chagrin and disappointment of his companion.

While he was still in Bayreuth, Grieg received a letter from Ibsen inviting him to visit him at Gossensass in the Tyrol. "You will be heartily welcome here, and I hope you do not make your visit too short. After the strenuous pleasures of Bayreuth you will certainly need some fresh mountain air, and that you will find up here." And so once the *Ring* cycle had completed its course, he and Paulsen made their way to the Tyrol. Paulsen described Ibsen as "taciturn and unapproachable – the soul of negation". Yet, although they never became close, Grieg seemed to establish some kind of rapport with him. Generally indifferent to music, Ibsen could on occasion be responsive. He was almost overcome on one occasion in Rome some years later when Nina sang a group of Grieg's Ibsen settings. "Just think of it," he told Beyer, in a letter of 19 March 1884 "after *Little Haakon*, and especially after *Album Lines* and *A Swan*, the icy exterior melted, and with tears in his eyes he came over to the piano where we were, and pressed our hands without being able to say anything." Grieg had longed to collaborate with Ibsen on an opera and after their meeting in 1876 Ibsen had toyed with re-fashioning his play, *Olav Liljekrans* as a libretto but never went so far as to send it to Grieg. And when they met in the early 1890s, plans for another opera on *The Vikings at Helgeland* were mooted but never came to anything, although Ibsen actually sent him the first act.

After leaving the Tyrol, Grieg made his way back north. He felt the contrast between southern Europe and life in Christiania more strongly than ever. He spoke of "icy coldness from every quarter", of difficulties with the orchestra, the only two bassoonists in the city were highly temperamental, and to raise money Nina and he made a trip to Sweden giving concerts in Stockholm and Uppsala. By 1877 Grieg's mounting frustration with life in Christiania where as he colourfully put it to John Paulsen, "the vilest cliques poison the air", came to a head. When the season ended and summer came, he upped and left. But it was not only the provinicial, straight-laced outlook of Christiania that was the problem, but a major artistic crisis that had been troubling him since the late 1860s. "Perhaps it surprises you," he told his friend, August Winding, "but if you only knew what an inner struggle I have waged these last years you would understand me. Every possible outer circumstance has prevented me from following my calling, and no one has been more dissatisfied with what I have achieved than I myself. ... I have lost the ability to manage the larger musical forms – and if one loses that, after once having had it, which I really did at one time – then it is farewell to the future." (Letter, 28 October 1877).

Grieg was drawn to the idea of living in the Hardanger region of the west country (Vestlandet). His impatience with life in the Tiger City, as Christiania was called because of its unfriendliness, had reached breaking point. He decided to uproot himself and leave. At the end of June 1877 he and Nina went to stay at Øvre Børve in Ullensvang a few miles from Lofthus, overlooking Sørfjorden and with the glaciers of Folgefonnen gleaming in the distance. It was idyllic and Grieg

Going to the Festspielhaus.

was blissfully happy, or as happy as he could be. He spent more time fishing than composing but the place he had rented was totally unsuitable for the rigours of the Norwegian winter. However rather than move to town, he decided to remain in the Hardanger country and so made their home at a small inn or guest-house in Lofthus. The Griegs did not actually live in the inn itself but in an adjacent building that had originally served as a store. They took their meals with the innkeepers, Hans and Brita Utne, with whom they became good friends. Some have hinted that in the latter's case, she and Edvard were more than friends, since several of Grieg's letters to her have remained outside the public domain. In later years the Griegs regularly returned to Lofthus every summer.

Grieg decided to have a hut built for him a little way from their home where he could compose undisturbed. It was to become known locally as "Komposten", a mixture of the words "Komponisten" (composer) and "kompost" (compost), an everyday part of the local farmers' life. Grieg had it built in September and October while he was in Bergen, and began putting it to practical use on his return. Whatever Grieg's feelings may have been at the beauties of the Hardanger country, there was no doubt about Nina's. It had long been no secret that for some time they had been growing apart. Grieg was 24 and Nina two years younger when they married and it was not long before the first euphoria of wedded bliss wore off. By the mid-1870s there was little real contact left between them and tensions had begun to surface. Those close to Edvard were urging him to try and talk things through with her. Nor was Nina's isolation in this remote rural community conducive to marital harmony. She was a person of spirit and temperament, and what had been the occasional bickering became more frequent and more strident squalls. Nina, it should be added, was not particularly interested in the usual feminine pursuits of her day. She found the mountain scenery oppressive and claustrophobic, and the prospect of actually settling there, as Grieg was at one time planning, appalled her. Small wonder that she fell victim to depression.

Nina was not the household muse, caring for the daily routine of domesticity. On the contrary she was in her element when the couple were "on the road", staying in good hotels, dining in reasonable style and meeting interesting people. In a sense her exclusive devotion as an artist to Grieg's songs, always travelling in his shadow, may have taken its toll on her spirits. In later years Grieg himself wondered whether an independent solo career would not have brought her more satisfaction – and ultimately greater marital harmony for them both. Whether she had the requisite gifts to sustain one remains a moot point but there is plenty of testimony to her gifts. Apart from her singing, she was a highly accomplished pianist. Indeed she sang *Haugtussa* to her own accompaniment on more than one occasion and made numerous appearances with her husband as a duo pianist. Some ten years later, in his *Autobiographical Account of a Foreign Tour in 1888*, Tchaikovsky wrote appreciatively of her. "In the first place she proved to be an excellent though not very finished singer; secondly, I have never met a better-informed or more highly cultivated woman, and she is, among other things, an excellent judge of our literature, in which Grieg himself was also deeply interested; and thirdly, I was soon convinced that Madame Grieg was as amiable, as gentle, as childishly simple and without guile as her celebrated husband". Tchaikovsky was right: her voice was essentially unschooled though she had taken some lessons early in her career. A fragment of her singing '*Solveig's Song*' without accompaniment recorded on cylinder in 1889 survives and though the sound is primitive in the extreme gives some impression of the purity of the voice.

Another critic, Joachim Reinhard, reporting for a New York paper, wrote, "Although it is easy to criticize Mrs Grieg's singing... no other vocal performance to this day has made such an impression on me as hers, and as far as I know, everyone who has had the pleasure of hearing her has felt the same. As soon as Mrs Grieg has begun to sing one forgets that one is in a concert hall. We suffer with her, we weep, laugh and rejoice with her from the beginning to the end." She evidently had the ability that all great artists must have of convincing the listener while they are performing that there is no other way of interpreting the music. To quote Grieg's younger contemporary, Christian Sinding, celebrated in his day among amateur pianists for *The Rustle of Spring*, "Tell me, why doesn't anyone else sing like that? Come to think of it, why doesn't everyone else sing like that? Because basically it cannot be otherwise. It is the only true way."

Against this background of domestic turbulence, Grieg was confronting his life's crucial artistic dilemma. When he is referred to nowadays as primarily a miniaturist, it is undoubtedly true that his most unique, and most inspired invention is to be found in the smaller forms, above all the songs and the *Lyric Pieces* for piano. Being a fine pianist Grieg naturally wrote both extensively and idiomatically for the keyboard, right from his earliest years. The ten books of *Lyric*

Pieces written over a period of 30 years, from 1868 through to 1898 are the staple diet of pianists the world over. But this should not be allowed to obscure the fact that in the G major violin sonata, op. 13 or the A minor piano concerto, op. 16, he was able to handle longer-breathed musical ideas and think in terms of paragraphs rather than sentences to commanding effect. But the concerto was the last work of any scale that Grieg had attempted and only three were to follow. Doubts have been voiced by later authorities in our own time, such as Gerald Abraham in his synoptic *Concise Oxford History of Music* or Donald Jay Grout in *A History of Western Music*: "The weakness in these works arise from Grieg's tendency to think always in two- or four-measure phrases and his inability to achieve rhythmic continuity and formal unity in long movements". Even so, Grieg's own self-insight and his acknowledgement of his artistic crisis is more poignant and eloquent for having been made at the time and from within, instead from the vantage point of a century later and from the outside.

"Day by day I am becoming more dissatisfied myself. Nothing that I do satisfies me, and although I think I still have some ideas, I can neither escape nor give form to my ideas when I proceed to the development of some larger project. It is enough to drive one to distraction – but I know well enough what the basic problem is. It is lack of practice, thus lack of technique, because I have never gone beyond composing by fits and starts. I am going to fight my way through the large musical forms, cost what it may. But that is going to stop now. If I go mad in the process, you will know why." (Letter to Matthison-Hansen, 13 August 1877)

Chapter 12

The G minor Quartet

It is against this background that the String Quartet in G minor, op. 27, came into being. It would seem that the first movement pursued a completely different course from the one we now know. There were two main ideas, the second related to the 'Temple Dance' in *Olav Trygvason*, both of which were later jettisoned. As its main theme and as a motif which binds the whole work together Grieg finally opted for the tune he had used in his song, *Spillemænd* (*The Fiddlers*), changing it from major to minor. There is no doubt as to its autobiographical overtones. Later in a letter to Holter, Grieg quotes some lines of Ibsen's poem. "It was the theme from this song (from 1876) that I used in 1877 in the string quartet. And in this, as you will understand, there lies a piece of personal history. I know that I had a big spiritual battle to fight, and I used a great deal of energy creating the first movement of the quartet there among the dark mountains of the Sørfjord in that summer and autumn." The last part of the Ibsen poem has particularly striking resonances.

I conjured the sprite of the waters,
He lured me to regions wide,
But when that dread sprite I had mastered
She was my brother's bride.
In mighty halls and cathedrals
I fiddled tunes refined,
But evil songs and horror
Were ever in my mind.

This has fuelled speculation in some quarters that Nina had taken refuge in John Grieg's arms during these crisis years or more accurately that Grieg himself believed that this might have been the case. In any event this lies firmly in the realm of conjecture.

When the String Quartet in G minor was complete in

February 1878, Grieg sent it to Robert Heckman whose ensemble, then among the finest in Germany, was to give the première of the piece in Cologne. A lengthy correspondence between violinist and composer took place. It is clear that Grieg not only adopted many of Heckman's technical suggestions but also made further revisions to the score before it was ready for its triumphant baptism on 29 October the same year at the Cologne Conservatoire. Heckman and Grieg also played the G major sonata, op. 13. Its performance at the Leipzig Gewandhaus the following month was anything but triumphal. The critic Edouard Bernsdorf was to prove a thorn in Grieg's side on practically every visit he made to Leipzig, and he ladled his vitriol unstintingly. "We have felt only displeasure and repugnance towards all the boorish and absurd stuff that is gathered together under the guise of a Norwegian national stamp, toward the mediocrity of the compositional inventiveness that lurks behind the rough-hewn and exaggerated Norwegian exterior (something non-Norwegians must accept in good faith), and toward the lack of any talent for structure and development – indeed, the lack of any ability whatsoever to create – adequately, without patchwork – a continuous whole in a movement (as here in the sonata and the quartet)." Grieg's mortification can be imagined. But as Sibelius once observed, no one has ever erected a statue to a critic: it is composers who count. And the words of Liszt which were reported to him must have lifted his spirits and given him the solace and encouragement he needed. "It is a long time since I have encountered a new work, especially a string quartet, that has interested me so strongly as this singular and excellent work by Grieg."

Of course, the String Quartet in G minor was not the only work that occupied Grieg during his time in the Hardanger country, even if it is the most important. Nor was it the only chamber work. As soon as he had finished the quartet and sent it to Heckman he set to work on a Piano Trio. However he finished only one movement (*Andante con moto*, CW 137) and well-fashioned though it is, the piece can hardly be described as vintage Grieg. But there are the fine *Improvisations on Two Norwegian Folk Songs*, op. 29 and *Den Bergtekne* (*The Mountain Thrall*), op. 32, for which Grieg himself had a particularly soft spot. While he was in Sørfjord, Grieg read Magnus Landstad's *Norske Folkeviser*, a collection of Norwegian folk ballads – and with evident enthusiasm, for it was one of them that provided the text for *The Mountain Thrall*. Scored for baritone, and the relatively unusual combination of two horns and strings, it is not dissimilar in theme to Keats's *La Belle Dame sans Merci*, and there are parallels, of course, with the scenes with the troll-king's daughter in *Peer Gynt*. A young man, wandering in the forest is bewitched by a giant troll's daughter as he passes near a runic stone. He loses his way and is pursued by trolls, a lone human in a hostile environment. Indeed, as Beryl Foster puts it in her book, *The Songs of Edvard Grieg*, it is 'more of a miniature cantata than a song'. Grieg himself wrote of it, "It is a glorious thought to be able to say here with Bjørnson: 'God knows that was written with devotion'. It is as if with this piece I have done one of the few good deeds of my life".

The Mountain Thrall is the first time that Grieg ventured into anything other than standard Norwegian – apart from the song *Millom rosor* (*Among Roses*). Landstad's *Norske Folkeviser* are folk-poetry that had remained faithful to its traditional roots. Generally speaking, Grieg was sympathetic to the use of *landsmål* or dialect language, which was still a controversial subject in Norway. In the long years when Denmark and Norway were one, the standard written language was Danish. This was differently pronounced in Norway but none the less allowing for local variations remained basically the same. When under the terms of the Treaty of Kiel in 1814, Denmark was forced to give up Norway, the language still remained Danish. As time went on the movement grew to modify the spelling of Norwegian so as to make it harmonise with the actual pronunciation. Both Ibsen and Bjørnson supported this movement as did many others including Henrik Wergeland, the most commanding Norwegian poet of the first half of the century. However by the mid-1850s a movement was gathering force to encourage a language based on those dialects deriving from Old Norse – in short *landsmål* or rural or country language. Since the late 1920s, this has been known as *nynorsk* or New Norwegian, and co-exists with standard Norwegian, *riksmål* (sometimes known as *bokmål* meaning written or literary Norwegian). In any event in the coming years Grieg was to turn for inspiration to two poets writing in *landsmål*, Aasmund Olavson Vinje and Arne Garborg, the former in his *Twelve songs*, op. 33 and the latter in *Haugtussa* (*The Mountain Maid*), op.67.

When Grieg left the Hardanger country in 1878 and took the String Quartet to Germany, his intoxication with its landscape had passed its peak. He settled in Copenhagen for some months in the early part of 1879, giving two concerts in the Danish capital, and on his return to Norway in May found that the old enchantment had faded. "For the first time here I feel the oppression of loneliness", he told Beyer. "The quietude

Grieg's song, Fyremål (The Goal) composed in 1880.

of nature is too cold for me after all the human feelings I have shared recently." In the autumn of 1879 there were concerts in Bergen, and he returned to Leipzig to play the Piano Concerto at the Gewandhaus. There were more concerts the following spring in Copenhagen and Christiania, all of which were sold out. But the sterility that every artist lives in fear of, had actually overtaken him. He had written virtually nothing. Naturally he was seized by the fear that this condition was permanent, that he had written himself out, and that his career lay in the past. Fortunately the muse was soon to revisit him.

In the spring of 1880 he was much taken with the poems of Aasmund Olavson Vinje who had died ten years earlier. For much of his life Vinje had been involved in journalism, writing serious, thought-provoking essays on literary and other themes. Grieg's *Twelve Songs to Poems by A.O. Vinje*, op. 33, must be numbered among his most poetic utterances for voice, and their intensity of feeling is unmistakable. Not all of the op. 33

95

set were actually composed in 1880; two were earlier, *Gamle mor* (*Old mother*) (1873) and *Langs ei å* (*Beside a stream*) (1877), though Grieg told his friend Paulsen that they were all written one after another in his childhood home on Strandgaten. Nor were there only twelve. Three others were composed but for various reasons omitted from the final collection. After the Vinje settings, Grieg was to compose no new songs for four years.

Two of the Vinje settings became specially well known. When Grieg became conductor of the Bergen Orchestra, the Harmonien, later in the year, he found that he needed new repertoire. He transcribed two of them for string orchestra as *Two Elegiac Melodies*, op. 34, changing their titles slightly. The first, *Hjertesår* (*The wounded heart*) was a transcription of op. 33, no. 3, in which the poet speaks of Spring and the pain it brings, while its companion, *Våren* (*The Last Spring*) has been called Grieg's most beautiful melody. The poem describes how the north is released from the icy grip of winter and adds a poignant note that the poet may be witnessing it for the last time. They rapidly took their place among Grieg's most popular pieces.

In the summer of 1880 Grieg decided that he really had had enough of life in the Hardanger region and by the autumn he was installed as conductor of the Bergen Orchestra. He remained there for two seasons in all, and under his leadership standards noticeably rose. The orchestra developed more responsiveness and greater delicacy and precision. Discipline was tightened. Grieg earned the obloquy of the philistine majority in the town when he enforced it by dismissing half of the female chorus for missing the final rehearsal of Handel's *Coronation Ode* in order to attend a ball. The press were completely baffled, so little did they understand what was required in an artistic enterprise. As his appearances as a pianist grew fewer, because of the demands made on his stamina – and with his respiratory problems, he found them onerous – he turned increasingly to the baton. It is obvious from contemporary descriptions that he drew playing of refined and multi-coloured sonority from the orchestra. Sir George Grove, founder of *Grove's Dictionary of Music & Musicians* (still the most exhaustive and comprehensive musical encylopædia in the English language) heard him a few years later. "How he managed to inspire the band as he did and get such nervous thrilling burst and such charming sentiment out of them I don't know. He looks very like Beethoven in face, I thought, and though he is not so extravagent in his ways of conducting, yet it is not unlike." Speaking of him in rehearsal, he said, "Such

Grieg's older brother, John, for whom he composed the Cello Sonata.

men cannot be judged by the standard of ordinary men – of Englishmen particularly. They are free from conventions which bind us, they are all nerves, they indulge in strange gestures and utter odd noises, and make everyone laugh till we find that that the gestures and looks and words are the absolute expression of their inmost feeling."

As time went on Grieg found the atmosphere at the Harmonien increasingly uncongenial. In December 1881 he wrote to a friend, "My health has improved so much that at least I have enough strength to conduct the orchestra. But I would not do it for another season for all the gold in the world. One is infected by all the pettiness and indifference that surrounds one. By next summer I will be a philistine and a provincial, but then if I am still living I will shake the dust off my wings." The chorus and orchestra sent him off in triumph. There was an orchestral fanfare, a laurel wreath and flowers and, as he told his friend, Matthison-Hansen, "when I came home, a pretty silver mug from the women's chorus. As a result I have become so cocky that no one can stand me".

During the 1881-82 season he had composed virtually nothing to speak of, due to his work with the Harmonien. But once he had given it up so as to devote himself to creative work, inspiration was slow in coming. He began a Piano Quintet 64 bars of which survive, and although its date is not known, it is possible that it comes from about this time. But the main work to consume his energies over the next year was the Cello Sonata in A minor, op. 36, written for his brother John. This in itself should have put paid to the speculation that had arisen a few years earlier at the time of the G minor Quartet. Work on it did not proceed smoothly and it was not until April 1883 that he put the finishing touches to the score. Perhaps in later years he was just a little harsh on it but generally speaking, he was not really far off target. Captivating though it is, the success of his 1882 Cello Sonata rather surprised Grieg himself. In 1903 he reproached his biographer Gerhard Schjelderup, "Of my larger works I think you are altogether too kind to my cello sonata. I myself do not rank it so high for it does not mark a forward step in my development." There are obvious echoes of the Piano Concerto in the first movement and the theme of the slow movement bears a close resemblance to the *Homage March* written for Bjørnson's *Sigurd Jorsalfar*. It does not add anything special to the repertoire in the way that either of the string quartets or the G major and C minor violins sonatas (opp. 13 and 45) do. Its first performance in 1883 was in Leipzig with Grieg at the keyboard and Ludwig Grützmacher as cellist.

The playbill for the première of *Parsifal* at Bayreuth in July 1882.

Grützmacher, incidentally, was one of the most celebrated virtuoso cellists of the day, and was himself active as a composer. He is remembered for his "transcription" of the Boccherini B flat Concerto, which was more or less the standard edition of the piece well into our day.

There is an explanation for the fact that after the Vinje settings of 1880, the outpouring of song dries up. Grieg always maintained that he composed with Nina's voice in mind but by 1883 the relationship with her had deteriorated to breaking-point, and in July he left her. It would appear that during the early 1880s he had come under the spell of a young admirer, Elise Schjelderup, an artist then twenty-six and living in Paris. (Her brother, Gerhard, himself a composer, was later to become Grieg's first biographer – in Norwegian at least.) It would seem that Grieg was planning to join her there, and during the coming months was taking French lessons, presumably, with that end in view. Their correspondence has never come into the public domain. In her book Beryl Foster points out that Grieg's periods of inactivity in this genre coincide with periods of estrangement with Nina. It is as if his muse was so dependent on the vocal quality she commanded – and he was close to no other singer – that she unleashed the springs of his invention and was the source of his inspiration in this field. There were only three songs in the period 1884-88

Liszt in his last years. Grieg found him looking "incredibly old… it was pitiful to see him".

and few in the early 1890s, though by this time Nina had given up singing in public. In any event when Grieg left Norway in July he was not to see Nina again for nearly eight months.

First he was off to Bayreuth for the world première of *Parsifal* by way of Thüringen where he collected a Belgian friend, the composer Frank van der Stucken. After Bayreuth the two stayed for a time in Rudolfstadt where Grieg spent his time practising the piano and taking French lessons from van der Stucken. His application for a travel grant to enable him to go to Paris had been turned down in Christiania, but that only increased his determination to get there under his own steam. A concert tour was his only means of generating the necessary funds.

He made an auspicious start at Weimar, where Liszt was still the Court Composer and Conductor. First, Grieg was the soloist in the Piano Concerto and then conducted the *Hofkapell*, the Court Orchestra, in the *Two Elegiac Pieces*. "It was simply marvellous to hear how they played them", he told Beyer. "Beautiful crescendos and pianissimos beyond one's wildest dreams and a fortissimo that was like a world of sound" (17 October 1883). He found Liszt "incredibly old... it was pitiful to see him", though the great composer would have been a mere 73, which may, of course, have seemed a huge age to 40-year-old eyes. But he never lost sight of his debt to the great composer nor forgot "how wonderful Liszt was to me" on this occasion, as he had been on earlier occasions. Then, Grieg went on to Dresden, Meiningen, Breslau, Leipzig, Frankfurt and so on, including among other things the new Cello Sonata in his recitals. After that there were several concerts in a number of Dutch cities.

All through this period he was in constant correspondence with his confidant, Frants Beyer in whose home Nina had by now taken refuge. It was Beyer's loyal and tireless mediation that was eventually to persuade Grieg to return to Nina. As the moment of truth drew near his resolve weakened and he put off his departure for Paris. Instead he stayed on in Amsterdam where he came to form another friendship that was to last for the remainder of his life – with Julius Röntgen, the Dutch violinist and composer. Röntgen's father had also been a violinist and at this time the young man was in his late twenties and Grieg twice his age. Julius became a professor at the Leipzig Conservatoire and leader of the Gewandhaus Orchestra before returning to Amsterdam to pursue a career as composer and conductor. In 1914, seven years after Grieg's death, he became director of the Amsterdam Conservatoire.

A portrait of Grieg by Leis (Elise) Schjelderup with whom Grieg was infatuated at this time.

Their friendship was to remain lifelong. Grieg stayed with Röntgen for the best part of three weeks – and the plan to go to Paris quietly dropped from view. Frants Beyer had been his trusted confidant throughout all these years, a trust that was well placed since he destroyed the most intimate of Grieg's letters, thus protecting his friend from prurient eyes. Nina wisely did the same.

Elise Schjelderup was probably not the first to captivate Grieg – and certainly not the last! As late as 1895 he was swept off his feet by the pianist, Bella Edwards, Danish in spite of the English surname, to whom he wrote a number of letters which leave no doubt as to his infatuation. He described himself as "a lovesick schoolboy who is blissfully giddy over the girl he loves!" He would have been 52 at this time, not a great age. Fame often serves as an aphrodisiac to the young but Bella Edwards though flattered was made of different stuff. Wiser counsels prevailed and Bella Edwards quietly but firmly disentangled herself from her admirer. She had studied at the Copenhagen Conservatoire in the mid-1880s and after her departure from Grieg's life, she went on to settle in Paris with her friend the violinist, Eva Mudocci. There she became a friend of the great Norwegian painter, Edvard Munch. She eventually settled in London where she lived until her death as late as 1954.

In their authoritative study Benestad and Schjelderup-Ebbe make the point that in Grieg's surviving letters, there are few endearments or much affection in his references to Nina, save for "a certain gratitude in his later years". But it would, of course, be a mistake to conclude on this evidence that there was no tenderness or warmth. A nature such as Grieg's, passionate in his profession of affection (as his letters to Beyer show), would doubtless have observed certain reticences concerning so central a relationship. Indeed deeper feelings sometimes do not call for overt expression. Beyer effected the reconciliation with Nina by dint of much persuasion and with great tact. There was no humiliating return to Norway to meet a wounded, reproachful but forgiving little wife. He proposed that the two couples should holiday together in Italy and that they meet in Leipzig in late January. This they did – and from there they slowly made their way to Rome. All went smoothly but, alas, Frants and his wife Marie had to return to supervise the building of his new home, Næsset, about five or six miles outside Bergen at Hop on Lake Nordaasvann. The Griegs stayed on in Italy remaining there for four months before making their way home.

The reconciliation was sufficiently complete for Grieg to

give thought to making a more permanent home for himself in Norway, and give up his itinerant lifestyle. No doubt inspired by Frants, he even considered building a villa alongside Næsset. But when that proved impractical, he decided to build one on a neighbouring plot of land called Trolddalen (the Valley of the Trolls). This he bought and the remainder of the year was spent on building their new home "Troldhaugen" (The hill of the trolls). Grieg spent 500 kroner on the land but the building costs spiralled to about 12,500 kroner, for which money had to be found. The size of the loan he had to raise naturally worried him, and the paradox soon arose of his having to resume concert-giving and its itinerant way of life in order to work off his debts, instead of composing in the surroundings of his new home. These practical concerns consumed so much of his energies that there was hardly time for composition. However, the fact remains that had inspiration come, it would have forced him to drop everything else.

These were on the whole barren years and the only real work of note from 1883-86 was the *Holberg Suite*, op. 40. 1884 was the bicentenary of the birth of the Dano-Norwegian playwright, Ludvig Holberg, popularly described as "the Molière of the north". His native city, Bergen celebrated the event by organizing a Holberg Festival. As Norway was then part of Denmark and Holberg gravitated to Copenhagen, he is considered Danish. For the bicentenary celebrations, Grieg wrote two pieces, a cantata for male voices designed to accompany the unveiling of the Holberg's statue and an instrumental work. When the cantata was given a second performance a few days after the unveiling, Grieg followed it by playing what has since become known as the "Holberg Suite". It was originally called *Fra Holbergs tid (From Holberg's time)*: *Suite*

Troldhaugen at Hop outside Bergen with Grieg's House.

in the olden style. Not long afterwards Grieg refashioned it for string orchestra and it is in this form that it is most familiar. Indeed it comes as a surprise to most music-lovers outside Norway that it began life in keyboard form. The original is very much a pastiche in the style of an eighteenth-century keyboard suite. It transcribes perfectly into the string orchestra medium, which enjoyed relatively little favour in the middle of the century. It was the appearance of the Dvořák and Tchaikovsky Serenades for strings and the *Holberg Suite* that restored its fortunes.

The year 1885 was not much more productive. Much of his working-time was committed to the thorough-going revision of the *Peer Gynt* music that he had long been promising himself, and for which the new Copenhagen production provided the pretext. He remained in Copenhagen through to the new year, playing his Piano Concerto at the end of January under the baton of his old friend and countryman, Johan Svendsen in the presence of the entire Danish royal family. By this time Svendsen had been in Copenhagen for a couple of years as conductor of what we know as the Royal Danish Orchestra (*Det Kongelige*) and their old rapport – or near-rapport – was rekindled. "I have a feeling", he told Beyer, "that Svendsen will end up in Christiania again; he is homsesick for Christiania and would like to have me there as well. We are together daily, and although I never really feel that I know him completely, I must say that he is more amiable towards me than ever. He often nearly reveals his inner self but then suddenly the shutters come down. Just between you and me, there is one thing that worries me – and I have said this in all candour to

The music room in Troldhaugen.

Svendsen himself: I am worried about his art, for his future as an artist. He has peculiarities of character which hinder the unfolding of his rich creative gifts. This upsets me so much that I could weep, for there is no one from whom I have expected greater things." (February 1885)

The Griegs remained in Denmark for the best part of the Spring, returning to Norway in May. In spite of Edvard's poor health they had made long concert tours visiting Aarhus, where they were snowed in for six days, Aalborg, Horsens and Ribe. Nina had sung, Grieg had played, both of them performed as duettists and in Aarhus he conducted an excellent string ensemble. The ardours of travel and playing, given the fact that with one lung his stamina was limited, saw to it that composition took a back seat. He managed to raise 2,000 Danish kroner from his tour to help pay for Troldhaugen.

Back in Norway for the summer he was able to turn to some of the small pieces he had sketched out in Denmark. Two of them, *Sommerfugl* (*Butterfly*) and *Liden Fugl* (*Little Bird*) were destined for inclusion in the next set of *Lyric Pieces*, op. 43 later that summer. He spent much of his time in the company of the Danish poet, Holger Drachmann and together they made a trip

107

to Hardangar and Lofthus and then stayed in a cottage in the Jotunheimen mountains. The visit lifted Grieg's spirits enormously and was obviously good for his health. He waxed lyrical, in a message to Beyer, about their "unbelievably glorious trip. Have become positively young again. And a new zest for work!!" The fruit of Drachmann's visit were some poems which he wrote specially for Grieg and which the latter published later that year as the *Rejseminder fra Fjeld og Fjord* (*Travel Memories from Mountain and Fjord*), op. 44. It had been many years since Grieg had made any settings of Danish, but it is only fair to say that Grieg scholars are noticeably unenthusiastic about them. Benestad comments tartly that it was not only Drachmann who was on holiday but his powers of self-criticism too. Nor do his next Drachmann settings, composed the following year, the *Six Songs*, op. 49 get a much better press, any more than the poems themselves.

But all these are small pieces. It had been some four years since he had produced a work on a larger scale. Now a new violin sonata, No. 3 in C minor, op. 45, was in the process of gestation, 20 years later than its predecessor. He had begun work on it at Troldhaugen before setting off for the Hardanger mountains with Drachmann, and it was this that occupied him for the rest of the year. By January 1887 the new piece was ready and awaiting its final coat of polish. Grieg played it to Frants Beyer that summer but was still not entirely happy with it. Its first performance was due in Leipzig that autumn and the first thing Grieg did on arrival was to run through it with his friend and countryman, Johan Halvorsen, then a 24-year-old student of Adolph Brodsky. Grieg wrote to Beyer, "I've just returned from the home of Professor Brodsky, Halvorsen's

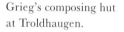

Grieg's composing hut at Troldhaugen.

Interior of Grieg's composing hut.

teacher. We played the new violin sonata together – the one you got such a poor impression of last summer. I was as disappointed then as you were, but tonight (albeit after changing the shortcomings) I experienced a joy that is seldom granted to an artist. He played it absolutely incomparably... it was indeed what I had intended, but I just didn't think my intentions could be made real."

Brodsky was in his mid-thirties at this time and was to lead a dizzy international career. Three years later he was to leave the Leipzig Conservatoire to lead Walter Damrosch's orchestra in New York, later going to Manchester to lead the Hallé from the mid-1890s and subsequently become Principal of the Royal Manchester College of Music. The performance was a great success and apart from anything else, laid the foundations for another friendship that was to last for life. Needless to say, the critic Bernsdorf laid into the new sonata, as he had the String Quartet in G minor. According to a letter Grieg wrote to Beyer, Bernsdorf actually hissed him and the Brodsky Quartet when they took a bow after a performance of his String Quartet in February the following year. But the piece has somehow survived both his and subsequent critical onslaughts, and has established a firm place in the repertory.

Chapter 13

The Famous Lunch

Grieg remained in Leipzig for some time, enjoying the company of his young compatriots, Johan Halvorsen and Christian Sinding, and the hospitality of Brodsky. At the turn of the year, on New Year's Day 1888, there was a gathering at the Brodskys that has become quite famous in musical history, when Brahms, Grieg and Tchaikovsky were all gathered under one roof. Brahms was rehearsing the newly-composed C minor Piano Trio, op. 101, with Brodsky and the two famous

The violinist Adolph Brodsky at whose home the celebrated lunch took place.

composers joined them for lunch together with another, who had yet to make her mark on the musical world, the young Englishwoman Ethel Smyth, then in her 30th year. Mindful of the many kindnesses he had received from him in the past, Grieg was quick to leap to Liszt's defence when Ethel Smyth was rash enough to venture some criticism of his music. Tchaikovsky recalled this celebrated lunch and described the impression Grieg made on him. It is the best portrait in words that we have of Grieg at this time in his life.

"As they were playing through Brahms new trio, a man walked into the room – very small of stature, middle-aged, extremely sickly in appearance, shoulders of uneven height, head covered with large blond, tousled locks. The facial features of this man, whose appearance for some reason

Johannes Brahms

immediately appealed to me, are not especially noteworthy; one cannot call them either handsome or unusual. But on the other hand, he has unusually attractive, medium-sized, sky-blue eyes of irresistibly charming character, eyes that remind one of an innocent, adorable child. I was glad in the very depths of my soul when, upon our being introduced to each other, it was revealed that the bearer of this inexplicably attractive exterior was a musician whose deeply-felt music had long since secured for him a place in my heart. It was Edvard Grieg." At the lunch itself, Nina was placed between Brahms and Tchaikovsky, but it was not long before she leapt up and said, "I can't sit between these two. I get so nervous." Whereupon Grieg said, "But I can!"

Along with Tchaikovsky's account of Grieg the man, he had this to say of Grieg the composer. "Perhaps Grieg's mastery is

Tchaikovsky in the year of his meeting with Grieg.

112

a good deal less than that of Brahms, the development in his music less elevated, the aspiration and goal less broadly conceived. A subconscious striving towards the unfathomable depths seems to be entirely lacking. But on the other hand, he is closer to us, he is more understandable and kindred precisely because he is so deeply human. When we hear Grieg we realise instinctively that this music was written by a man driven by an irresistible longing to give expression by means of sound to the stream of feelings and sentiments of a deeply poetical nature – without being a slave to a theory, to a principle, or to a banner hoisted aloft as a conseqence of this or that accidental circumstance of life – but rather yielding to the prompting of a living, sincere artistic feeling. Perfect form, cogency and flawless logic of thematic development we shall not find in the music of the renowned Norwegian (although the themes are always fresh and new, coloured by the characteristic features of indigenous Teutonic-Scandinavian nationalism). On the other hand, what enchantment, what spontaneity and richness there is in the musical invention. What warmth and passion in his singing phrases, what a fountain of pulsating life in the harmonies, what originality and entrancing distinctivness in his clever and piquant modulations, and in the rhythm as in everything else – how endlessly interesting, new, original!"

We know that Grieg responded with equal warmth to Tchaikovsky, and invited him to come to Norway and stay with him. And when later on he received a telegram from the famous singer, Désirée Artôt, inviting him to a supper party in Berlin at which Tchaikovksy would be present, he did not hesitate for a moment but left instantly for the capital. The following evening he went to the concert at which Tchaikovsky conducted *Romeo and Juliet*, the First Piano Concerto with Aleksandr Siloti as soloist, the *1812 Overture*, some songs and two movements, the Introduction and Fugue from the First Suite, and went to dinner with him at a restaurant afterwards. When he returned to Leipzig the day afterwards he felt as if the whole thing had been a dream. He wrote to Beyer later that month, "In Tchaikovsky I have gained a warm friend for my music. He has as much affecction for me as I have for him, both as an artist and as a human being. You will come to know him because he will undoubtedly come to Troldhaugen." (Letter, 29 January 1888).

Later that year the great Russian composer was instrumental in procuring an invitation for him to conduct in Moscow and St Petersburg, though Grieg was never actually free to take up this offer. In later years, after Tchaikovsky's

Grieg and Nina in 1888.

death, he was to write both perceptively and sympathetically to his friends August Winding and Frants Beyer about the great Russian composer. To the former he wrote on the last day of 1895, "You speak of Tchaikovksy's *Symphonie pathétique*? And God help you if you have not rejoiced in it! Is it not remarkable! Though I have to use my powers of reflection to understand the unity in the whole work, yet all four movements have genius. It is so wholly Tchaikovksy and so altogether masterly." And he wrote to Beyer on 6 January 1906 that he was struggling in the evening with an English translation of Tchaikovsky's *Life and Letters* by his brother Modest. He speaks of his nobility and adds, "It goes to my very soul. Often it seems as though I were looking into my own. There is so much I recognise in myself. He is melancholic – almost to insanity. He is a fine and good person – but an unhappy one. The last I did not realise when I

114

met him some time ago. But it is so: one has either oneself or others to contend with."

Ethel Smyth was not the only English composer Grieg met in Leipzig. This was also the period in which Delius entered his life. Frederick (still known at this time as Fritz) Delius, had come to Leipzig to further his studies in 1886. He had a strong temperamental affinity with Scandinavia and with Grieg's music even before they met. His father, a wool-merchant had sent him to Sweden in 1881, when he was 19, to represent the family business, but as Lionel Carley, our foremost authority on Delius, puts it, he "slipped the leash" of the plain, practical manufacturing town of Norrköping and was off to Norway. By the time he met Grieg, he had become fairly fluent in Norwegian and was quite besotted with Norway. Indeed he had already set some Norwegian poems by Bjørnson, Welhaven and others, published as his op. 5. In Leipzig Delius had been befriended by Christian Sinding, and it was when they were out for a walk one day that Sinding spotted the Griegs and introduced them. Their bond, like that between Tchaikovsky and Grieg, was immediate and enduring. We soon find Grieg

The Norwegian composer Christian Sinding.

writing enthusiastically of him, describing him to Beyer as "Norway mad", having been there four times already and "camping out on the heights of the *Hardangervidda* (Hardanger plateau) for a fortnight at a time". It was not long before he became known in their circle as the *Hardangerviddeman*. Delius was among the guests at an hilarious Christmas Eve party at the Griegs, at which everybody became very merry, and Sinding managed to set the Christmas tree on fire before knocking it over.

Not only Delius but another great composer and pianist was in Leipzig at this time, namely Ferruccio Busoni. Brahms had provided him with an introduction to Reinecke with whom he was now studying. When Grieg introduced him to Delius, it was with the words "This is a most remarkable pianist – and perhaps something more!" Grieg was enormously happy during these months in Leipzig and in later letters often referred with particular delight and nostalgia to those days. Only one grey cloud hovered on the horizon – his forthcoming debut in London, which he was dreading.

The opening of Grieg's song, *Det først møte* (*The first meeting*) to a poem by Bjørnson in Grieg's own hand and dated February 1888.

Chapter 14

Grieg goes to England

Although Grieg had conquered Germany (with the notable exception of Edouard Bernsdorf, of course), he had yet to make a personal appearance in England. His reputation, though, was well enough established. Eduard Dannreuther had given the first performance of the Piano Concerto in London as early as 1872 and repeated it four years later. A somewhat lofty review of the latter makes bizarre and entertaining reading.

"[Dannreuther]... played with an earnestness and artistic finish which indicated that he estimated the work at a higher value than the majority of his auditors... we cannot say that

London in the 1890s: Hanover Square with St George's Church on the left.

definite themes are wanting in the Concerto but many of them are uncouth – the first, especially, with the ascent of two augmented fourths in consecutive bars – and they appear thrown together... Occasionally we have some excellent writing and the orchestration is exceedingly effective in many parts, but the composition left a sense of weariness upon the audience which somewhat checked the well-merited applause which the executant received at the conclusion of his difficult task."

Grieg had been invited to London in 1884 by the Royal Philharmonic Society but was decidedly underwhelmed by the fee on offer and pleaded ill-health. But as his début on 3 May 1888 drew near, his nerves grew apace. From Leipzig he wrote to Beyer, "I've already reported sick once before, so that won't work and I don't know of any other way out. The *Hardangerviddeman* [Delius] suggested that I tell them that an old aunt of mine has just died! That's just like him." But, of course, nerves were eventually overcome, and a St James Hall concert at which he played the "uncouth" Concerto under the baton of Frederick Cowen marked the beginning of what was to prove a special and enduring a relationship with the English musical public. Apart from his appearance as a soloist, he also accompanied Nina in some songs and conducted the *Two Elegiac*

118

Melodies, op. 34. What struck him with singular force about the English orchestra was the sheer quality of the strings, which numbered almost sixty. "There were times when one could weep for joy, it sounded so wonderful." Before long plans were afoot for a return visit the following year, this time a more extended one. Even Bernard Shaw who affected indifference to Grieg's charms, thought him an altogether outstanding conductor. "Grieg is so successful in getting good work out of the band that if the directors were wise, they would get him to take it in hand permanently." A few days later Grieg gave a recital with Wilhelmine Neruda, who was about to become the wife of Sir Charles Hallé. Their programme included the F major sonata, op. 8 and the last two movements of the new C minor sonata, op. 45. The Griegs then went on holiday to Ventnor on the Isle of Wight. On later visits they ventured to St Leonards-on-Sea near Hastings where Grieg's English publisher, George Augener had a rather plush bolt-hole. While

SEVENTY-SIXTH   SEASON, 1888.

PHILHARMONIC SOCIETY

UNDER THE IMMEDIATE PATRONAGE OF

Her Most Gracious Majesty the Queen,

THEIR ROYAL HIGHNESSES THE PRINCE AND PRINCESS OF WALES,
THEIR ROYAL HIGHNESSES THE DUKE AND DUCHESS OF EDINBURGH,
THEIR ROYAL HIGHNESSES THE DUKE AND DUCHESS OF CONNAUGHT,
THEIR ROYAL HIGHNESSES THE PRINCE AND PRINCESS CHRISTIAN,
HER ROYAL HIGHNESS THE PRINCESS LOUISE (MARCHIONESS OF LORNE),
HER ROYAL HIGHNESS PRINCESS MARY ADELAIDE (DUCHESS OF TECK),
HIS ROYAL HIGHNESS THE DUKE OF CAMBRIDGE,
HIS SERENE HIGHNESS THE DUKE OF TECK.

FOURTH CONCERT, THURSDAY, MAY 3, 1888.

ST. JAMES'S HALL.

Doors open at Half-past Seven o'clock. To commence at Eight o'clock precisely.

✦ Programme. ✦

PART I.

PETITE SUITE, "Jeux d'Enfants" ... ... *Bizet.*
(First time in England.)

CONCERTO in A minor, Pianoforte and Orchestra ... ... *Grieg.*
MR. EDVARD GRIEG.
(His first appearance in England.)

LIEDER { *a.* "Erstes Begegnen" } ... ... *Grieg.*
       { *b.* "Farewell to Tvindehougen" }
MISS CARLOTTA ELLIOT.

TWO ELEGIAC MELODIES for Stringed Orchestra ... ... *Grieg.*
(First time at these Concerts. Conducted by the COMPOSER.)

PART II.

SYMPHONY in C (No. 6) ... ... *Mozart.*
AIR, "Il est doux" (Hérodiade) ... ... *Massenet.*
MISS CARLOTTA ELLIOT.
OVERTURE, "Ruy Blas" ... ... *Mendelssohn.*

CONDUCTOR .. .. MR. FREDERIC H. COWEN.

Programme bill of Grieg's first concert appearance in England.

he was in London, Grieg performed a great kindness and service for his new English friend, not dissimilar from the one Liszt had performed for him nearly 20 years earlier. He succeeded in persuading Delius's father, who had so long resisted his son's ambitions, to allow him to leave the family business to pursue a musical career.

Troldhaugen turned out not to have been the permanent round-the-year home of which Grieg had spoken a few years earlier. In order to pay for it, he had to take to the road. No sooner was their visit to London over than the couple were off to Copenhagen for the first Scandinavian Music Festival where Grieg was to have conducted the Piano Concerto with Eugene d'Albert as soloist. In the event, the Norwegian pianist Erika Lie-Nissen, a friend of Nordraak's, stood in for him. The Griegs spent a couple of months at Troldhaugen before Edvard, this time in the company of Frants Beyer, crossed the North Sea for a second time to give concerts in Aberdeen and Birmingham. In the land of his forefathers and only 50 miles or so from their ancient ancestral birthplace, Grieg conducted the Overture, *In Autumn*, op. 11, which he had revised and reorchestrated for the occasion, and the *Holberg Suite*. Again he was made aware of the enormous popularity his music enjoyed. He had received a three-minute standing ovation in London before playing a note, and his welcome outside the capital was hardly less rapturous.

The invitation that had been mooted while he was in London for an extended return visit soon came. As he said in a letter to Delius, "I would rather stay at home but Troldhaugen begs me for some pounds sterling!" Soon his financial worries were to be resolved. His income from concerts soon increased handsomely, while Dr Abraham, the head of his Leipzig publisher, Peters, on learning of the debts with which Grieg had burdened himself, arranged for a "loan" from Peters to pay them off – a loan, which was, to all practical intents, a gift as the composer was never asked to repay it. Abraham's munificence was well placed for Grieg was himself a man of great generosity. At the end of the decade his friend Frants Beyer ran into difficulties and was even considering selling his home Næsset, that had inspired Grieg to build Troldhaugen. When Grieg heard the news he wrote, "It was a heart-rending letter! I cried like a child! No, it just cannot be allowed to happen. For here I sit and I am saying (to quote one of Brorson's hymns) 'O, my Sulamit, All that I have is also yours!' And at this moment I have more than I need. Must I tell you, dear Frants, that everything I own is at your disposal! It would make me unhappy if you did not take me up on this – indeed,

I'm afraid I would think less of you than I always have. If you
finally decide that you must absolutely sell Næsset, well, then
one of two things will happen: either I will also sell
Troldhaugen or else I will be at the auction when Næsset is
sold!" Beyer was not the only friend who could bear witness to
Grieg's instinctive generosity. In 1904 he made a substantial
gift to Matthison-Hansen, his Danish friend from his
Copenhagen days, and he was also good in this respect towards
his relatives.

Early in 1889, Grieg was in Germany to conduct the Berlin
Philharmonic but by the middle of February he was back in
London after a spell in Leipzig. He played the F major violin
sonata, op. 6, with Wilhelmine Neruda, now Lady Hallé, and
the Cello Sonata, op. 36 with Alfredo Piatti ("as boring as he is
famous", as Grieg put it), and the new C minor violin sonata,
op. 45 with Joseph Joachim, the greatest violinist of the day for
whom both Brahms and Dvořák had written their concertos.
Later the same month he went to Manchester where Sir

Charles Hallé, now a septuagenarian, played the concerto under Grieg's baton. Piano-playing in public was becoming increasingly burdensome to Grieg. Only a few weeks before his London debut he told Beyer, "Chamber music and small pieces don't bother me, but when I try to use a sledge-hammer on the piano I don't achieve the intended effect but only destroy myself." And so, after the 1880s he gave up playing the concerto in public. When the *Musical Times* published an appreciation of him in October 1907 after his death, it recalled Grieg's 1888 performance of his piano concerto which "added further beauty to that inherently captivating work. Ah, how feelingly he played the lovely *Adagio* – and as a strong contrast, with what vitality and energy, what rhythmic drive he played the last movement with its free-flowing Nordic melodies". A glimpse of the sheer intensity and poetic refinement of his playing in the recordings can be caught on a collection of CDs on the Norwegian label Simax, which is devoted to him and his early interpreters, both pianists and singers. His first were recorded on his eventful visit to Paris in 1903, and he made some piano rolls in Leipzig in April 1906.

In all there were eight concerts in five weeks, at which Nina, despite less than robust health, sang several of his songs, and played the *Norwegian Dances*, op. 35 with him. Among the audience at some of these was "Corno di Bassetto", the pseudonym which disguised George Bernard Shaw. When Shaw had gone "to hear Mr Grieg at the Popular Concerts on Saturday", he had found the room "filled with young ladies, who, loving his sweet stuff, were eager to see and adore the confectioner" – that, interestingly enough, a decade earlier than Debussy's *bon mot* about pink sweetmeats filled with snow. A few days later he returned to the subject of Grieg, noting with a characteristic Shavian flourish: "His sweet but very cosmopolitan modulations, and his inability to get beyond a very pretty snatch of melody do not go very far with me; for I despise pretty music. Give me a good, solid, long-winded classical lump of composition with time to go to sleep and wake up two or three times in each movement".

From London Grieg went to Paris to see Édouard Colonne, the conductor whose name survived so long into our times, thanks to the *Concerts Colonne* that he founded in the 1880s. Grieg's cause had not made quite such headway in France as it had in Germany and England, and in the early 1880s his name was virtually unknown, this in spite of the fact that both Svendsen and Bull had been active in the French capital. However both Saint-Saëns and Lalo, in particular with his

Rhapsodie norvégienne, had stimulated interest in both Norway and Grieg. The Lamoureux Concerts had included the Piano Concerto in their programmes in February 1885 and Saint-Saëns' pupil, Arthur de Greef played it during the 1889 Exhibition in Paris under Grieg's direction. It was this and the production of *Peer Gynt* at the Théâtre du Châtelet in 1894 that marked Grieg's real breakthrough in France.

During 1888 Grieg had corresponded energetically with Delius, who had earlier suggested that they spend some time together in Paris. Instead Grieg invited him, Christian Sinding and George Augener to Troldhaugen for the summer, from which at the end of July they set off on a tour of the mountains in Jotunheimen. This was another period of great happiness on which Grieg often dwelt with nostalgia and although he and Delius corresponded with regularity in later years, they never

The Joutenheim

subsequently spent so long in each other's company. One of Delius's letters to Grieg strikes a strong resonance. Writing from St Malo before his visit to Troldhaugen, Delius said, "My instinct has seldom led me astray, my reason often. When I first met you it was no longer instinct for I had already been acquainted with you so long through your music. I believe nothing reveals a human being so openly as music. A poet can (probably) dissemble but a composer must show himself, or nothing at all." Grieg was an intuitive composer *par excellence*.

Chapter 15

The 1890s

In 1891 ideas for his last essay on a larger scale, a second string quartet, in F major, began to surface in his mind. Indeed, more than surface, for he completed the first two movements, after which inspiration refused to flow. Although the thought continually plagued him, he never managed to put the remaining movements into a finished shape. In a letter to Adolph Brodsky written four years later, on Christmas Day 1895, he refers to "that damned string quartet which constantly lies there unfinished like an old Norwegian cheese". Later in the first years of the new century, and in his 60th year, he could speak of his continuing struggles with it. "These last years have brought so much misery, both physically and spiritually, that I wasn't in the mood to proceed with this cheerful work – quite the opposite of op. 27. But I hope to find the long-sought tranquillity and inclination this summer". And three years later, barely twelve months before his death he wrote despairingly to Brodsky, "If only I could at least finish the string quartet for you". After his death Nina sent the two movements and the sketches that remained to his Dutch friend Julius Röntgen who was at first doubtful about them but soon changed his mind, and now though they are rarely performed in public, they have been recorded. It is evident that Grieg's powers of self-criticism, fuelled no doubt by his complex about his ability to think in large-scale forms, got the better of him. Both the movements that survive are vintage Grieg, thoroughly characteristic and fully worthy of him. The scherzo is quite captivating. There have been various attempts to put the remaining sketches into performing order – and a conjectural completion has been commercially recorded. Röntgen's friendship endured well beyond the grave for not only did he rescue the two movements of Grieg's Second String Quartet but the 1878 Piano Trio fragment from oblivion and in 1930 published a Grieg biography a couple of years before his own death.

In 1890 Grieg had yet to reach 50 but thoughts of mortality and of his advancing years were beginning to trouble him. You must remember that the average expectation of life in the nineteenth century was much lower than it is in our own time. By the first years of the 1890s, Brahms was in his late 50s and only a few years later (in his early 60s) was to be captioned in photographs as "Brahms in old age"!

Of course his vulnerable health cannot have enhanced his spirits. In November 1890 Grieg and Nina had gone to Copenhagen where he remained until April 1891. He checked in at his usual haunt, the King of Denmark Hotel, but immediately became an invalid. He was unable to take food and was completely drained of vitality. "Am exhausted and out of sorts. The weather is awful. Everything is awful. Under such circumstances it is doubly good to know of a distant but true friendship", he wrote to Beyer on 12 November 1890. Three months later he returned to thoughts of mortality. "I won't say that I'm afraid of either life or death but there is one thing I am afraid of: to look at myself and note that I am growing old – that the ideas of the younger generation will sail out on expeditions the meaning of which I do not fully comprehend. In a word I fear the possibility of losing the capacity to feel what is true and great in the outposts of the spirit that move steadily forward throughout one's lifetime. For that reason I have – now more than ever – an instinctive need to know all the nuances that move steadily forward in the intellectual life [of our time]. If one now allows anything of significance to glide by without having assimilated it – before one knows what is happening, it will become a power that one doesn't understand, because one hasn't followed that which is new from the very beginning. To be left lying half forgotten on the road as time marches across one's sinful cadaver – that seems to me the greatest wretchedness that can befall a person. And with how countless many does this not happen? Perhaps with most – but they don't know it and are quite happy. It is different with the artist. When he becomes a part of the reactionary forces, he is lost."

He stopped work on the new quartet in March and left Copenhagen for Christiania. There were plans for an ambitious *Peace Oratorio* to a text by Bjørnson but these came to nothing. In May the Griegs returned to Troldhaugen where they remained for the summer. Röntgen and his family went to Norway and stayed in Lofthus where Grieg and Nina joined them and together they set off for the Jotunheim. It was on this journey in which they were joined by Beyer that they heard some of the remarkable folk song that flourished, untarnished by contact with the outside world. Nowadays when it is impossible to go to any part of the world however remote, without finding ethnic music adulterated by the all-pervasive phenomenon of western pop, it is difficult to imagine the impact this must have made. At Skogadalsbøen they found a 19-year-old, Gjendine Slaalien, who was singing a lullaby which Grieg subsequently included in his *Nineteen Norwegian Folk Songs*, op. 66, calling it *'Gjendine's Lullaby'*. Grieg remained in contact with her until his death and she lived on to a great age – in fact until her 100th birthday in 1972.

The 1890s and the first years of the twentieth century saw Grieg's lifelong interest in folk music increasingly deepen. The summer of 1891 acted like a shot in the arm. The result was the *Lyric Pieces*, op. 54, which he dedicated to Röntgen and which includes the extraordinary *Klokkeklang* (*Bell-ringing*). A few years later the conductor Anton Seidl orchestrated four of them including *Bell-ringing*. Prompted by this, Grieg himself decided to orchestrate them replacing *Bell-ringing*, which he thought too radical, with *Gjætergut* (*Shepherd Boy*) as the *Lyric Suite*. Grieg was not the only one to find *Bell-ringing* too modern. The editor of the *Musical Times*, writing in 1892 speaks of it thus: "Grieg writes a bare fifth instead of a single bass note so constantly that our ears have become as accustomed to the ugly succession of these, as to the Twelfth stop of an organ; but when he gives us, as he does in his latest work, a piece in which both hands play nothing but bare fifths throughout, we begin to feel that the whole foundations of musical science are being undermined and a state of artistic atheism is spreading in our midst. If one needs confirmation of this misgiving one has only to look at the compositions of young France and Italy, when he will see an open defiance of all harmonic tradition [that is] absolutely appalling."

In the autumn of 1891 Grieg made a successful appearance in Christiania, where he conducted the first performance of the *Peer Gynt Suite No. 2*, op. 55. He had given his very first concert in Christiania in 1866, 25 years earlier, and the event was turned into a great celebration. There was a torch-light procession by the students, and a banquet at which Ibsen was also present. But Grieg was not deceived by its blandishments and still judged the Norwegian capital harshly. "I don't think they can yet tolerate true artists among them – for long. When we just drop in and then hurry off again, everything is honey and roses. But there is still too much uncivilised coarseness and civilised pettiness here"

A few days earlier Grieg made his first appearance, as it

were, as a political agitator, albeit a mild one. Among his numerous accomplishments Grieg was a fine orator and at a meeting of the Student Society in Christiania he took the opportunity to argue the case in favour of the removal of the union symbol from the Norwegian flag. This was greeted with great nationalist fervour by the audience and drew a letter of approbation from Bjørnson.

At this time fortune seemed to be smiling on him. The torch-light procession had been like nothing he had ever experienced before, and basking in his successes he returned home to Bergen and Troldhaugen. But not long after his homecoming he was stricken with influenza, and subsequently rheumatism. His spirits plummeted and his appetite for work was naturally affected. He did succeed in re-fashioning the incidental music to *Sigurd Jorsalfar* expanding the "Homage March" and providing it with its brief introductory brass fanfare. Indeed such was Edvard's health that the Grieg–

Krøyer's famous portrait of the Griegs.

Delius correspondence was conducted by Nina rather than Grieg himself. She comes across as charming, touching even, and occasionally a trace coquettish.

On 11 June, 1892, Grieg and Nina had been married for a quarter of a century, and they celebrated their silver wedding anniversary in style. Although Grieg did not want to make a fuss, his circle of friends and admirers – and indeed the whole of Norway – decreed otherwise. As the day approached, so his apprehension mounted. It was a day that he was never to forget. The morning brought with it good weather and as they went into the living room, they scarcely recognised it. They were greeted by a sea of flowers, countless gifts and 150 telegrams, and there was Frants Beyer presiding over it all. Outside the house, the Bergen town band played a chorale and Grieg lost his composure and cried like a child. Over 100 visitors called to pay their respects at about noon and when he was presented with a special book from his Danish friends, it also taxed his emotional equilibrium. And the festivities went on into the evening, as he wrote to Röntgen, there were songs, speeches, fireworks, cannons, Bengalese lights and bonfires. The fjord was filled with boats, and apart from the 150 guests at supper, the train to Hop brought some 5,000 people to Troldhaugen, and the couple were serenaded by 230 singers. His friends in Bergen presented him with a Steinway grand – which is still to be found in Troldhaugen – from Christiania came the Werenskiold portrait now in the National Museum in Stockholm.

By the autumn, the couple returned to Christiania where Grieg conducted the first performance of the *Sigurd Jorsalfar* music. Then they went on to Copenhagen, Berlin and Leipzig, where on 7 February 1893 he conducted the *Peer Gynt Suite No. 2* and the Piano Concerto. The soloist was the young Russian virtuoso Aleksandr Siloti, whom Grieg had heard playing Tchaikovsky's B flat minor concerto in Berlin. He was no less a virtuoso than his cousin, Sergei Rachmaninov and a keen champion of new music. His career continued well into the 1920s and 30s when he settled in the United States.

In the spring Grieg continued to be plagued by health problems. In the end he was forced to cancel his proposed trip to England in May to give some concerts in London and go on to Cambridge for the conferment of an honorary degree. Dr Abraham generously took the couple on a tour of southern Europe ending at Menton, then a smaller town than it is now, on the Côte d'Azur. Here, it would seem, Grieg recovered enough to compose the sixth set of *Lyric Pieces*, op. 57. His poor health enabled him to escape from any 50th birthday celebrations and he spent the day quietly at the Grefsen Spa in Christiania to which he had been ordered by his doctors.

In November he was back in Copenhagen conducting the Piano Concerto with another legendary pianist Teresa Carreño. She had the distinction of being the third and fifth wife of the same man, the pianist-composer, Eugène d'Albert, another great exponent of the concerto. But Grieg was not the only one assailed by health problems. Nina had been suffering from a kidney complaint that was to prove sufficiently serious to entail hospital treatment. She was detained for several weeks and only discharged in late November. Her constitution was not seriously weakened: she survived her husband by the best part of three decades, living until she reached her 90th birthday in 1935.

It was in June 1895 that Grieg first encountered the poetry of Arne Garborg, and it was this that was to give rise to one of

Grieg as conductor.

his greatest works, the song-cycle *Haugtussa* (*The Mountain Maid*), op. 67. Garborg's collection of the same name had only appeared two months before in April, so was hot off the presses. It comprised some seventy poems and it quite captivated Grieg. Its background was the "desolate farming country of Jæren to the south of Stavanger as Garborg could recollect it from the time before pietistic revivalism had invaded the neighbourhood. That life was both earthy and exuberant, hardly touched by Christian conceptions or morbid broodings over the soul, sin and damnation". He found its nature mysticism irresistible and wrote that the poems in *nynorsk* or *landsmål* were so rich in verbal music that all that remained was to write it down. So completely was he under its spell that he threw himself into the settings with an almost feverish intensity and within only a matter of two or three weeks had completed twelve songs. But then something strange happened. Whether or not he was doubtful as to their quality or their acceptability to the wider musical public is unclear, but he put them on one side for three whole years. At one time he planned to turn it into a work for voice and orchestra but something still kept him from publishing the songs in the form in which we know them. Twelve months later in June 1896, he wrote to Röntgen, "*Haugtussa* slumbers on. I haven't touched it since Christmas when it was sung to you. Of late I have been lyrical [an allusion to the *Lyric Suite* which he had just scored]... Can't you cure me of this illness? What I want to compose doesn't get composed, and what I don't want to compose does. A dreadful illness!"

The songs did not finally appear until two years later in 1898 when Grieg published the eight we know. There are others which he decided against including, perhaps feeling them of lesser quality or alternatively feeling that the cycle would perhaps be too long. And it is as a cycle that they should be performed and evaluated. Although Grieg was to return to the medium in two sets of songs to words by Otto Benzon in 1900, *Haugtussa* remains his last major achievement in the field.

At much the same time Grieg wrote one of his most popular and rewarding scores, the *Symphonic Dances*, op. 64. This he composed in September 1896 for a medium that flourished in the nineteenth century but has fallen out of fashion in our own times – namely the piano duet or as it is widely known in Europe, piano four hands. He immediately set about orchestrating them but strangely enough, progress was slow. In fact it was not until two years later that they were ready and they did not receive their first performance until February 1899

Edvard and Nina Grieg with Dr Max
Abraham, his publisher (left), and
the pianist, Oscar Meyer in Menton.

in Copenhagen under the baton of his old friend Johan Svendsen. To a certain extent he was modelling the work on the example of Svendsen's own *Norwegian Rhapsodies*. The thematic ideas derive from Lindeman's collections of folk music: the first includes a halling from Valdres, the second a halling called *Heste-byttaren* (*The horse-trader*), and so on. A halling is a sturdy folk-dance in 3/4 time, a solo male dance. Grieg had used a couple of these tunes earlier on in the *Norwegian Folk Dances*, op. 17. Grieg was adamant that the four should be performed together and wrote to his German publisher in no uncertain terms. "To publish the *Symphonic Dances* individually – for such a thing I can't find a German expression that you would want to hear. If, for example, you published the second piece on its own, you would thereby ensure that the whole set would perhaps never be performed! If I were ever to perpetrate a symphony, perhaps you would publish the scherzo by itself. Well, why not?" And he goes on more presciently than he can have realised, "In the new century many Gordian knots from the preceding century will be untied! In the end man himself will be divided up, and liver, lungs and heart – each separately – will be offered for sale." Be that as it may, many commentators have felt the *Dances* less than *Symphonic*. In his book *A Hundred Years of Music*, Gerald Abraham was pretty dismissive of Grieg's structural thinking. "Technically Grieg was far from being the equal of Smetana, much less of Dvořák, Borodin or Tchaikovksy. The Piano Concerto, and the sonatas are essentially salon music put under a microscope – and the last of the sonatas, the C minor for violin and piano, is structurally the most feeble of all; even the *Symphonic Dances*, fine as they are, are a long way from being genuinely symphonic." The repeated sections certainly reinforce this impression and Grieg himself felt so, and in 1900 asked for many of them to be omitted. Symphonic or not, they are enchanting pieces and scored with a delicacy and imagination that Grieg had only come to command in later life.

If the summers were spent idyllically, the autumn and winters were usually spent "on the road". It was only in the 1920s that international copyright protection became a reality, in part due to the efforts of Richard Strauss. Before that Grieg's income, and that of any other composer, was derived from the sales of his printed music. Once the music was sold, it could be performed without further payment. His remaining means of support derived from concert appearances. Naturally the long periods of illness Grieg suffered took their toll on his ability to perform. "Sluggishness, weakness, shortage of breath, lack of energy – these are my major achievements", he once told Beyer after a bout of pneumonia kept him in Copenhagen and prevented him from giving concerts in Weimar and Berlin in the spring of 1895. Later that year he went to Leipzig where he stayed for some months at the invitation of his publisher, Dr Abraham, where he heard the Fourth Symphony of Brahms.

Grieg admired Brahms's music enormously and although opportunities of hearing it were obviously fewer than they would be in our days of broadcasting and compact discs, he studied the scores as they appeared and played through the piano arrangements that came out. He particularly admired the Piano Quintet in F minor, op. 34. Moreover, their earlier encounter in Leipzig, at which Tchaikovsky was present, would seem to have laid the foundations for a good personal relationship. "Last week", he wrote to Beyer in 1895, "we were frequently with Brahms in Leipzig, where he was staying for a few days, and it was a great pleasure to be together. I don't understand how such a one-sided person as Brahms – one-sided in his greatness, I mean – can appreciate my music which, so far as I can see, goes in a very different direction. But reticent though he is, he let me know that he does appreciate it. His Fourth Symphony was performed in the Gewandhaus under Arthur Nikisch. It's a work I didn't know before, and its first movement is one of the most beautiful things he has written. Generally speaking, however, he admired the earlier more than the later Brahms. The Brahms symphony was not the only work to make a strong impression on him during these months. A little earlier he had heard César Franck's oratorio, *Les Béatitudes* which he described as "a piece written by a master so great that, in my opinion, no one now living can measure up to him".

He was with Brahms a great deal later in March 1896 when he went to Vienna where, as Grieg picturesquely put it, "they taverned together". "He was jovial and friendly. I can't say the same for Dvořák, with whom, however, I made only a superficial acquaintance. Then I visited old Bruckner, a trembling greybeard, but touchingly childlike", he wrote in a letter to Iver Holter (28 March 1896). Grieg succumbed to bronchitis when he was in Vienna later that year to conduct at the Musikverein and during that time Brahms called on three occasions to inquire after his health, though he himself was far from well. He lunched Grieg and Nina at his favourite restaurant, *Der rote Igl* (The Red Hedgehog) and went with them to the concert. Indeed, unusually for him, he remained throughout the concert which was in fact Grieg's first appearance at the Musikverein.

The Viennese audience were enraptured and delighted. Brahms even attended the reception afterwards, at which according to Röntgen, Grieg spoke not a word of his own triumph that evening but paid tribute to Brahms. He spoke with such warmth and eloquence that the great man sat with his head bowed and after the speech came over to Grieg, much moved and pressed his hand without saying a word. Grieg himself wrote to Halvorsen about the orchestra "You should have heard those strings!! And such people – such a city! Happiness, the capacity to get excited, good will, spontaneity. They are in a class of their own."

Grieg went to a new year concert at which Brahms's String Quintet in F major, op.111, was given only a few months before that master's death. The couple remained on the continent for the winter of 1897 but on his way back to Norway in late April Grieg had the honour of conducting the Berlin Philharmonic in Copenhagen in his Piano Concerto with Ferruccio Busoni no less as the soloist. Nina had become unwell during the spring (breast cancer was suspected) and had not accompanied him to Vienna though she was well enough to join him in Copenhagen. They spent the summer quietly in Troldhaugen and Lofthus.

During the last years of the century Grieg travelled as widely as his health permitted. In Sweden he gave some highly successful concerts, all sold out, at the Royal Opera in Stockholm in the autumn of 1896. At a banquet given in his honour at the Grand Hotel attended by 300 distinguished guests, he made a firmly patriotic yet conciliatory speech that clearly inspired an audience which was obviously concerned about the gradually deteriorating relations between Norway and Sweden. From there he went back to Vienna where he conducted the Piano Concerto in which Busoni was again the soloist. The beginning of 1897 found him in Leipzig and then the Netherlands where the Concertgebouw Orchestra under its founder-conductor, Wilhelm Mengelberg gave a concert in his honour. There was time for some creative work and while in Copenhagen during the spring he worked on the orchestration of the *Symphonic Dances*, op. 64.

It was in the autumn of 1897, that Grieg was drawn into the planning of what was to be the first Bergen Festival. The Norwegian economy had expanded and prospered during the century and an exhibition of Norwegian trade, industry, arts and crafts had been planned in Bergen for the summer of 1898. Without any thought as to the consequences Grieg invited the Concertgebouw Orchestra and Mengelberg for the whole festival. The consequences were not slow to emerge. It was, of

Grieg, a studio portait
taken in Amsterdam.

course, agreed that the Bergen Orchestra was not of international standing but the feeling was that a Norwegian festival should feature Norwegian musicians, and the committee had intended to engage the Christiania Orchestra. On hearing of his move the whole committee resigned but the die was cast, for Grieg had set his heart on exposing the Bergen public to the sonority and ambience of a great orchestra and he himself resigned in turn when his wishes were disregarded. In the end after a good deal of unpleasantness, the Concertgebouw Orchestra was engaged. Their concerts stimulated a public clamour in both Christiania and Bergen to do something about the quality of their own orchestras. However strong feelings had stirred and it was some time before they died down, so much so that even six months after the festival Grieg could speak of Christiania being full of bile and venom, "enough to make a witches' brew for a whole generation".

Much of the autumn was taken up with travel. Grieg gave no fewer than ten concerts in Britain during the course of October and November and in early December played at Windsor Castle for Queen Victoria. "I'm not keen on court affairs as you well know," he told a Danish friend, "but this was something different. The queen is sweet if you can say this about an elderly lady. She knew almost all the programme, enjoyed Nina's singing in Norwegian, and asked for more. Everything was natural and genuine. She spoke about *Peer Gynt* and would have liked to hear *The Death of Aase* and *Last Spring* for string orchestra." In fact on her death in 1901, Grieg was approached to write a coronation march for Edward VII but he declined.

For all his republicanism Grieg seems to have enjoyed a rapport with royalty. He was received by the Kaiser Wilhelm on his yacht Hohenzollern when he anchored off Bergen in 1904 and appears to have got on famously with him. But Grieg perceived himself as a man of the left. His sympathies had been very much with the revolutionary communards in Paris in 1870-71 and like Bjørnson, he voted for Sverdrup and the liberals in 1873. He detested the Tsar, though he never met him. After the brutal suppression of the 1905 uprising in St Petersburg, he wrote to Brodsky saying, "We Norwegians never kiss! But I would willingly make an exception for all of the wretched, persecuted Russian people. I wish that I could place a bomb under the Russian government and administration, starting with the Tsar. They are the worst criminals of our time."

Chapter 16

Last Years

A glance at Grieg's opus list will show that this last decade or so of his life was dominated by the piano. True, there are the settings of the Dane, Otto Bentzon, not a great poet perhaps but then they are not great songs either with the exception of one or two, like *Lys nat* (*Translucent night*). This song captures some of the magical atmosphere of the white summer nights of the North that make these latitudes so special. There are also a couple of orchestral transcriptions, *Aften på Højfjeldet* (*Evening in the mountains*) for strings, oboe and horn, and *Bådnlåt* (*Cradle Song*) – and the valedictory *Four Psalms*, op. 74 , for mixed voice choir and baritone solo. Grieg's religious beliefs in later years were very much shaped by his encounter with a distant relative Johann A.B.Christie on his visit to England in 1888. Everything

Bergen at the turn of the century.

points to the fact that Grieg had a deeply religious nature. He broke more or less completely with the organised Christian Church and found himself in sympathy with the less dogmatic Unitarianism that he encountered in Birmingham on this 1888 visit. Unitarianism itself believes in one God and rejects a number of central Christian tenets, particularly the divinity of Christ. Both Edvard and Nina joined the Unitarian Church at this period. As Grieg wrote in a letter to Christie, "I believe in people, and I believe in God, and I still believe that the God who created them has something good in mind for them. Otherwise I would not wish to live a second longer."

Myllargutten, the hardanger fiddler who inspired Grieg's *Slåtter* or *Norwegian Peasant Dances*.

But it is the extraordinary keyboard works, the *Slåtter* or *Norwegian Peasant Dances*, op. 72, written in the first years of the twentieth century and the *Stimmungen* or *Moods*, op. 73, which stand out. Whatever its perceived limitations, there is much greater range in Grieg's piano music than is commonly realised. The ten books of *Lyric Pieces*, the last of which appeared in 1901 as op. 71, are far more than the teaching material so fondly imagined by some musicians. Many of them are miniature tone-poems of great refinement. Grieg himself was in no doubt as to the originality of the *Norwegian Peasant Dances* or the *Nineteen Norwegian Folk Songs*, op. 66, from 1896, the period of *Haugtussa*. Grieg told Röntgen of having "put some hair-raising chromatic chords on paper. The excuse is that they originated not on the piano but in my mind. If one has the Vøringfoss beneath one's feet, one feels more independent and daring than down in the valley". The fourteenth of the *Folk Songs*, op.66 is the source of the theme Delius used in his much played tone picture, *On hearing the first cuckoo in spring*.

Grieg had long been fascinated by the hardanger fiddle music which he had encountered and the transcriptions he made of them are boldly and powerfully imaginative. They are harmonisations of hardanger fiddle tunes in which Grieg, as he put, it was "trying to express the hidden harmonies in our folk music". The *hardingfele* (hardanger fiddle) is a folk violin from western Norway, which generally has four strings above the fingerboard and four or five wire sympathetic strings below, and characteristic national decoration. The *Slåtter* are full of character and make no attempt to "prettify" this repertory as any comparison between them and the original hardangar melodies will show. Some of them almost sound like Bartók. They are easily his most searching and stylistically innovative keyboard pieces. Small wonder that they attracted Bartók to pay a visit to Norway some years after Grieg's death. There's a story of how in the 1890s, while he was in Paris, Ravel had played one of his *Lyric Pieces* to Grieg. Grieg stopped him and said "You should see the peasants at home with the fiddler stamping in time with the music" – and how Grieg then got up and skipped across the floor with surprising agility to demonstrate the point. It is this robust side of Norwegian folk music which surfaces in these pieces.

The *Slåtter* into which Grieg had poured his soul, did not meet with the success they deserved in Norway. He played six of them at a concert in Christiania in March 1905. "What hurt me, was that the *Slåtter* did not strike home as they should have. I played them with all the affection and magic I could muster. But – where my evolution as a composer has led me, I don't have my own people with me, and that is hard to bear." To be fair though, they received a more positive response a few days later but few Norwegian pianists really took to them. Grieg was delighted and astonished that the young Australian pianist-composer, Percy Grainger played them with such idiomatic feeling and that they were also enjoying a success in France.

On his first long visit to Paris late in 1889 Grieg had conducted the Colonne Orchestra in the *Peer Gynt Suite* and *Bergliot* as well as the Piano Concerto with Arthur de Greef as soloist. Grieg scored an enormous success with the French public and made a number of influential friends among the musical establishment – notably, the composer Vincent d'Indy though he never met Debussy. Despite the jibe Debussy made about Grieg's music reminding him of "the taste of pink sweetmeats filled with snow", he was much influenced by Grieg in his String Quartet in G minor, and it went further than that. Some years after Grieg's death he modified his generally unfavourable response and went so far as to include one of Grieg's violin sonatas in a recital he gave with Arthur Hartmann which was otherwise exclusively devoted to his own

Grieg at the piano.
He recorded a few piano pieces in Paris in 1903 and 1906.

music.

Apart from the Debussy Quartet, French music of the period owed much to Grieg. On one occasion Delius went so far as to assert in Ravel's presence that "modern French music was Grieg and Grieg alone, plus the prelude to the third act of Wagner's *Tristan*". The great French composer is said to have nodded in assent, "*C'est vrai. Nous sommes toujours très injuste envers Grieg.*" ("That's true. We are always very unjust towards Grieg".) Doubtless it was his natural sympathy for the composer that prompted Ravel to choose the Grieg Concerto for his graduation piece at the Paris Conservatoire.

Although an enthusiasm for all things Norwegian (and in particular Ibsen's plays) had gripped France in the 1890s, Grieg's relations with the French public were soured at the turn of the century as a result of his public utterances on *l'Affaire Dreyfus*. The Dreyfus Case had polarised France during this decade and had brought to the surface an ugly seam of anti-semitism. Alfred Dreyfus was an officer of Jewish origin in the French Army who had been unjustly accused and subsequently convicted of treason for selling military secrets to the Germans in 1894. Such was the outrage the case aroused that the author Émile Zola was prompted to publish an open letter to the President of France entitled *J'accuse*. Although there was ample evidence of his innocence offered at his appeal five years later, the conviction was upheld. So strong were the feelings aroused both inside France and abroad, that when in 1899, Édouard Colonne wrote again inviting him to conduct another concert of his own music at the Théâtre du Châtelet, Grieg felt so outraged that he turned it down. "While I thank you for your kind invitation," he wrote, "I greatly regret to tell you that, in view of the outcome of the Dreyfus appeal, I cannot agree to come to France at this time. Like all non-Frenchmen, I am so indignant over the contempt with which law and justice are treated in your country that I could not bring myself to perform for a French audience. Forgive me for my inability to feel otherwise and try and understand me." Egged on by Bjørnson who, like Zola, was active on Dreyfus's behalf, Grieg allowed this letter to be made public and within days it had received international publicity and prompted a surge of nationalist feeling among the anti-Dreyfussards. He received threats and anonymous letters including one addressed "to the Jewish composer, Edvard Grieg".

The first few weeks of 1903 found him resting at Voksenkollen in Norway but in March he was back on the road, first to Copenhagen and then Prague where he was given a

The programme of Grieg's guest appearance at the Concerts-Colonne at the Théâtre Chatelet in Paris on Sunday 19 April 1903.

CONCERTS-COLONNE
THÉÂTRE DU CHATELET

Dimanche 19 Avril 1903, à 2 h. 1 4
(Vingt-Quatrième et dernier Concert de l'abonnement)
SOUS LA DIRECTION DE M.

EDVARD GRIEG
AVEC LE CONCOURS DE Mme

ELLEN GULBRANSON
du Théâtre de Bayreuth
ET DE M.

RAOUL PUGNO

EN AUTOMNE, Ouverture de concert, op. 11..... ED. GRIEG.
   (1re Audition).

TROIS ROMANCES avec accompagnement d'orchestre... ED. GRIEG.
   a) Berceuse de Solveig (Ibsen).
   b) De Monte-Pincio (Bjornson).
   c) Un Cygne (Ibsen).
   Mme Ellen GULBRANSON.

CONCERTO EN LA MINEUR pour piano, op. 16   ED. GRIEG.
   I. Allegro moderato.
   II. Adagio.
   III. Allegro, presto, maestoso.
   M. Raoul PUGNO.

DEUX MÉLODIES ÉLÉGIAQUES.............   ED. GRIEG.
   Pour instruments à cordes.
   D'après des poésies norvégiennes de A. O. Vinje.
   a) Blessures au cœur.
   b) Dernier printemps.

A LA PORTE DU CLOITRE (1re Audition)........   ED. GRIEG.
   Poème de Bjornson pour soprano et alto soli,
   Chœur de femmes, orchestre et orgue (op. 20).
   Mme Ellen GULBRANSON.
   Mlle CLAMOUS.
   Chœur de Nonnes.

PEER GYNT, 1re suite d'Orchestre (Op. 46)......   ED. GRIEG.
   Musique pour le poème dramatique de Ibsen.
   I   Le matin.
   II. La mort d'Aase.
   III. La danse d'Anitra.
   IV. Chez le Roi des Montagnes (Les Cobolds poursuivent Peer Gynt)
   Sous la direction de M. Ed. GRIEG.

LE CRÉPUSCULE DES DIEUX............   R. WAGNER.
   Scène finale (Mort de Brunnhilde).
   Brunnhilde : **Mme Ellen GULBRANSON.**
   Sous la direction de M. L. LAPORTE.
   PIANO PLEYEL

CE PROGRAMME EST DISTRIBUÉ GRATUITEMENT
Prière de ne pas entrer ni sortir pendant l'exécution des morceaux.

welcome worthy of a crowned head. Indeed his visit to the city was one of the great triumphs of his life. There were concerts of his major works everywhere throughout Bohemia and he was left in no doubt of the affection in which he (and all that he stood for) was held. There were long ovations and demonstrations. Teresita Carreño, daughter of the celebrated Teresa Carreño, was the soloist in the Piano Concerto. Grieg told Beyer (1 April 1903), she "roams brilliantly over the keyboard like a wildcat but there is poetry in everything she does". Dvořák's daughter, Magda sang some of the songs – in Czech – and he enjoyed his meetings with her father "It was fun to get closer to Dvořák. He is quite a character... to put it mildly. But very endearing". It is quite clear that his feelings were reciprocated for when Grieg sent Magda a letter of condolence on the death of her father she responded, "Your visit to Prague will always be among the most beautiful moments in my life, and it makes me so happy that you have remembered me. My father always talked about you with the greatest affection and the sound of your name is dear to us."

These heady days in Prague were almost matched when he proceeded to Warsaw, but Paris, of course, was another matter. Here he was to conduct the Colonne Orchestra on 19 April 1903, his first appearance in the French capital since the Dreyfus affair. It was during this period, while he was in Paris that he recorded some of the most popular *Lyric Pieces* and the slow movement of the Sonata, op. 7. Passions still ran high after the Dreyfus affair and various hostile elements in the press urged people to demonstrate. When Grieg walked on to the platform, the claque booed and catcalled, *A la porte*, à *la porte*. Grieg put down his baton left the platform and waited in the wings for the noise to subside. This it did, only to resume when he returned to the podium. He lifted his baton and plunged the orchestra into a fortissimo silencing the trouble-makers. The police threw the worst of them out of the hall. The concert was a great public success but not a critical one, with the sole exception of the composer Gabriel Fauré writing in *Le Figaro*. Grieg was an admirer of what he knew of Fauré's music and wrote that his review had shown his nobility of heart.

Unaccustomed, perhaps, to the more rumbustious style of criticism that you find in big cities, Grieg was hurt by Debussy's review of the concert in *Gil Blas*, which he thought personal. Throughout his life he received a pretty fulsome press everywhere he went. Bernsdorf was the sole exception during a period of thirty years. He did not see GBS's reviews nor would he have seen the 1874 review of Dannreuther's performance of the concerto. It was on this Paris visit that Debussy spoke of his Norwegian colleague looking like a photographer from the front and a sunflower from behind! However Grieg did not allow his artistic judgment to be swayed by this when he was discussing Debussy's music. In a letter to M.D. Calvocoressi (of 2 May 1903) he said, "It has been very interesting for me to read through his three *Nocturnes for orchestra*. Considerable talent and unusual inventiveness are expressed there, and I am very grateful to you for giving me an opportunity to become acquainted with this work. I hope to be able to have it performed in Scandinavia. With respect to *Pelléas et Mélisande* I will not presume to make a judgment merely on the basis of the piano score. I hope to hear the opera in Berlin. Obviously I see in this work as well the deep seriousness that inspires this artist. It is precisely this seriousness – which he mistakenly claims to be absent from my music – that attracts me to him and that I myself strive for in my work." Later on, some months before his death, he records in his diary, "to get acquainted with Debussy certainly was, for a connoisseur like me, to discover a truly tasty morsel. He spins a brilliant web of orchestral sound." He is speaking of the *Prélude à l'après-midi d'un faune*. "Wonderful harmony, completely unconventional but genuinely felt – albeit overdone".

In 1903 Nina experienced difficulties with her ears that troubled him greatly. He told Beyer on 20 January 1903, "I wish so much that I could say that things are going better here at home. But alas! Now I too am beginning to have my doubts. I fear for her hearing. The result of the treatment of these idiot doctors – specialists and non-specialists alike is of late – and daily – increasing her deafness. It is hopeless. I feel like crying as I write this. Think what music means for Nina, think what it means for the whole of our life together... God knows whether these Norwegians are not too brutal for such a delicate art as ear treatment... 'I could shoot them!' as my pious and gentle father always said."

In June came his 60th birthday celebrations which were on a scale that matched and perhaps even exceeded his silver wedding anniversary in 1892. The festivities lasted three days:

Bjørnson and Grieg at Troldhaugen in 1903.

A reception at Troldhaugen on Grieg's 60th birthday.

the newspaper *Bergens Tidende* paved the way by publishing a Grieg Edition and there were numerous concerts. There was a huge reception at Troldhaugen on the day itself and Johan Halvorsen and the Christiania Orchestra came to pay tribute. Later in the day there was a banquet at Bergen's Grand Hotel. There were countless press comments. One New York critic, writing in the *Musical Courier* summed up the paradox of nationalism in music by saying, "It is stupid to reproach Grieg with being too national. Had he been less so he would not now be universal". It is indeed the composers with the deepest roots in their own musical tradition, such as Chopin, Mussorgsky, Janáček, Vaughan Williams and others, that become the most universal.

Norwegian national feeling had reached fever point by the early years of the present century. As Ingvar Andersson put it in his classic survey, *A History of Sweden*, the union had been hastily and imperfectly effected, and there were tensions as the two countries had different types of constitution. In the 1880s

Norway had established a real parliamentary system and managed its own internal affairs, but foreign affairs for the union were handled by Stockholm and so Norway did not enjoy separate representation abroad. Separate consular representation became an increasingly important issue, particularly in view of Norway's advances in trade and shipping. This was the first Norwegian demand ahead of a separate foreign minister and an eventual dissolution of the union. Feelings on both sides grew high and the Norwegians began to

The programmes for Grieg's 60th birthday concerts in Bergen.

Nationaltheatrets Orkesters
Koncerter
i Bergen 15. og 16. Juni
i Anledning af
Edvard Grieg's 60-aarige Fødselsdag

Program til første Koncert:

1. Hyldningsmarsch af Sigurd Jorsalfar.
2. Koncert for Piano med Orkester:
   a) Allegro moderato.
   b) Adagio.
   c) Allegro marcato.
   Fru *Elisabeth Hals-Andersen.*
3. a) Det første Møde } for Strygeorkester.
   b) Vaaren
4. a) Henrik Wergeland, for Baryton og Orkester.
   b) Den Bergtekne, for Baryton, Strygeorkester og 2 Horn.
   Hr. *Ingolf Schjøtt.*
5. Per Gynt Suite No. 1.:
   a) Morgenstemning.
   b) Aases Død.
   c) Anitras Dans.
   d) I Dovregubbens Hal.
   Samtlige Kompositioner af Edvard Grieg.

Til Bergen
Digt af *Bjørnstjerne Bjørnson* — Musik af *Johan Halvorsen*
synges af *Ingolf Schjøtt.*

Program til anden Koncert:

1. *Sinding:* Rondo infinito.
2. *Grieg:* ›Brudefølget drager forbi‹
   instrumenteret af *Johan Halvorsen.*
3. *Halvorsen:* Musik til ›Kongen‹:
   a) Efter Mødet i Adelsklubben
   b) Forspil til anden Akt
4. *Svendsen:* Karneval i Paris.
5. *Grieg:* Koncertouverture: ›I Høst‹.
6. *Beethoven:* Ouverture til ›Leonore‹ No. 3.
7. *Liszt:* Ungarsk Rhapsodi.
8. *Wagner:* ›Valkyriernes Ridt‹ af ›Valkyrien‹.
9. — Forspil til ›Lohengrin‹.
10. — Ouverture til ›Tanhäuser‹.

Koncertflygel af Brødr. Hals's Fabrik (Haugens Pianolager).

make defensive preparations along their lengthy border with Sweden. Needless to say, as in all such circumstances when feelings run high, a "war party" soon emerged in Stockholm, and the Swedish Riksdag, or parliament, voted a huge credit of 100 million Swedish kronor for military purposes. Grieg was actually constrained to write at the height of the crisis to both the Kaiser and the King of England voicing his concern at the possibility of hostilities and asking them to mediate. Neither replied. Relations were very strained and Grieg himself wrote of the increasing hostility towards Norway and Norwegians. Bjørnson's plays were banned and Grieg's own music was hissed. After the negotiations collapsed the Swedish prime minister Boström resigned and the Norwegian Storting took the initiative and adopted a new consular law. When the King vetoed it the Norwegian government resigned en masse. This the King refused to accept and declared that he could not form another. In the resulting confusion the Storting assumed the monarchy, and with it the Union, ceased to function. The resulting constitutional crisis was only resolved by the Treaty of Karlstad which formalised the *oppløsning*, dissolution or literally "breaking-up" of the union. One of its provisions was the dismantling of the Norwegian fortifications along the border, which led many of the more fervent nationalist to feel that the treaty was a sell-out. Almost immediately a constitutional referendum was held on whether Norway should be a republic or a monarchy. The Storting approached the Danish prince Haakon to assume the throne, and though Grieg's instincts were predominantly republican, he supported the move.

In the last two years of his life, Grieg kept a diary which gives a fresh, natural picture of his day-to-day life. It begins on

Bjørnson, Nina, Karoline Bjørnson and Grieg.

the day that Haakon assumed the throne. He liked Haakon and his English-born queen, Maud: "If they are as unpretentious and natural and unaffected as they seemed to be, then we may dare hope for a democratic monarchy". When he was in England the following year he was asked to visit King Edward VII to convey the new king's greetings but the monarch committed the discourtesy of talking while Grieg was playing. Emulating Liszt's example before Tsar Nicholas ("Even music herself must be silent when His Majesty speaks"), Grieg stopped. When he subsequently recounted this episode to Haakon, the Norwegian king tried to soothe his ruffled feelings by saying, "But King Edward is the kind of man who can very well listen to music and carry on a conversation at the same time." To this Grieg responded, "That may well be possible (which it isn't) but all the same it is not permissible even for the king of England, and in justice to my art I cannot overlook it".

After the *oppløsning*, Grieg spent a lengthy period in Christiania until he set off on his travels in April 1906. To judge from his diary, he would seem to have had some fear that it might be his last journey. Ambitious it certainly was, taking in Copenhagen, Berlin, Leipzig, Prague, Amsterdam, London and Hamburg. His lifelong impatience with Christiania resurfaced: "If I had to work here, I would go out of my mind". As he had found earlier in his career, educating the public was an uphill struggle. They were "so stubbornly conservative that they wouldn't even come to the concert at which Halvorsen conducted Richard Strauss's *Tod und Verklärung*". Grieg's admiration for this tone-poem, which moved him to tears, is well-known but it did not extend to *Also Sprach Zarathustra* let alone *Salome*, "which lasts almost two hours but it seemed like seven".

He may have heard *Salome* but unfortunately he missed the performance of Delius's opera, *Village Romeo and Juliet* in Berlin. By this time Delius was well into his forties and Grieg must be forgiven for thinking his lack of success betokened lack of creative development. Unfortunately he died before Delius began to gain the recognition to which his gifts entitled him. And in the absence of performances and publications Grieg's knowledge of his old friend's music remained scanty. However he was to encounter a new friend from the English-speaking world, Percy Grainger. During his visit in May to England he was widely fêted and received an honorary degree at Oxford. He gave three concerts, playing the Cello Sonata with no less an artist than Pablo Casals ("incomparable, a great, great

The composer and pianist, Percy Grainger, an outstanding interpreter of the Grieg concerto in the early years of the 20th century.

artist"), and at one of these concerts Grainger served as page-turner. Grainger also played to Grieg and his playing bowled him over. After hearing him he wrote of "wonderful Percy Grainger, who turned pages for me at the concert, and whom I love as if he were a young woman. It is a dangerous thing to be greatly admired, but when one admires in return, as I do here, it all evens out. I've never met anyone who *understands* me as he does. And he is from Australia."

His enthusiasm was sustained throughout this year for twelve months later, after Grainger had visited Troldhaugen, he noted in his diary, "I had to become 64 years old to hear Norwegian piano music interpreted so understandingly and brilliantly. The way he plays the *Norwegian Peasant Dances*, (the *Slåtter*, op. 73) and folk song arrangements, breaks new ground for himself, for me and for Norway. And then this enchanting, natural, profound, serious and childlike naturalness. What a joy to gain a young friend with such qualities" (27 July 1907). There is a charming picture taken the day before this diary entry which shows Grainger with the Griegs and with Julius Röntgen.

When the time came for Röntgen to return home, Grieg said that he felt they would not meet again. There could be no denying that Grieg's health was failing: he could not sleep without fear that he would choke, and breathing was increasingly difficult. Grainger he naturally hoped to see as he had not cancelled plans for another concert appearance in England, hoping that the concerts would in fact serve a

149

therapeutic purpose. He was persuaded to go into Bergen and stay at the Hotel Norge and even went so far as to organise clothes for the trip. But it soon became clear that there would be no trip; his condition rapidly deteriorated and on 4 September he drifted into a coma. Nina was summoned but by the time she had arrived he was dead.

The funeral brought tributes from kings and other heads of state; Röntgen and Brodsky both came, the latter playing in the orchestra under Johan Halvorsen. And after the wreaths were laid, the *Funeral March for Rikard Nordraak* was played. Grieg, it appeared, carried the *Funeral March* with him on his last concert tour in case he should die abroad. Frants Beyer, faithful friend as ever, saw to it that his ashes were finally returned to Troldhaugen where they were placed in a grotto in the cliff. Nina remained at Troldhaugen for a time but came to spend more and more time in Denmark where she eventually settled. She obviously moved in musical circles as Sibelius mentions having sat next to her at a lunch party when he was in Copenhagen to conduct the Seventh Symphony in September 1924, when she was nearing eighty. For all the anxiety about her health in 1890s she lived to be nearly ninety, dying in 1935.

Grieg's popularity continued unabated right up to the late 1940s and 1950s before it underwent a temporary decline and then surged to its present level. His achievement is not in question. He may not belong among the very greatest masters but the fact remains that despite his relatively small output, he is probably a figure of greater substance than either Glazunov or Granados to go no further than his neighbours in the alphabet. But Grieg shares one quite special quality with one of

In the garden at Troldhaugen in 1907 (from left to right) Grieg, Percy Grainger, Nina Grieg and Julius Röntgen.

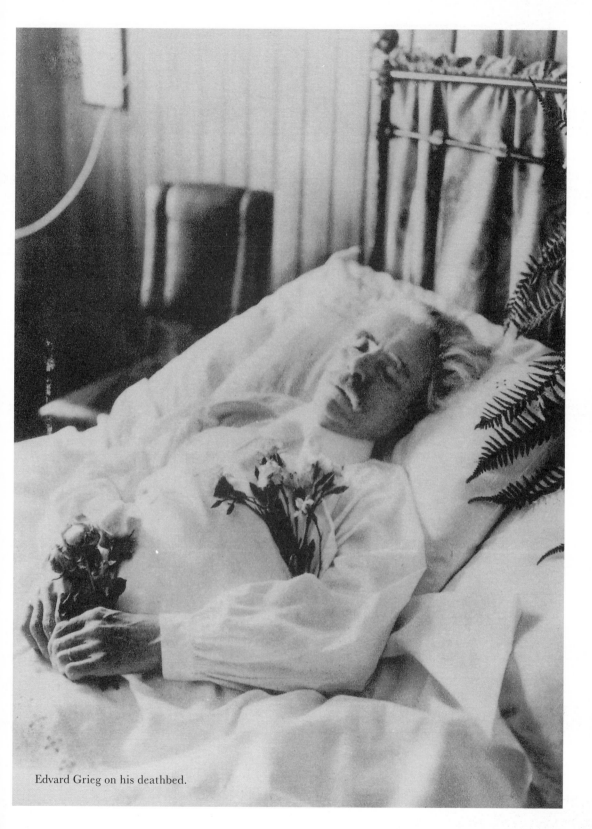

Edvard Grieg on his deathbed.

the great masters, namely Schubert. He has a naturalness of utterance that is totally disarming, and a melodic freshness that should (but, as we have seen, inevitably doesn't) silence criticism. His music never strikes poses; there is a complete absence of artifice and pretension. It is content to be what it is. If music is a report on your inner experience, something that you cannot say in words but only in music, his is a totally truthful and complete one, which comes straight from (and goes to) the heart. In this lies the secret of his universal appeal.

On his death Grieg's reputation stood high, and throughout the early part of the century, he maintained the high profile he had enjoyed in his lifetime. "Morning Mood" from *Peer Gynt* was not just the introduction to Grieg for many schoolchildren in Britain and North America, it was pretty well the introduction to music itself. The Piano Concerto enjoyed enormous exposure. The songs and the piano music were frequently featured in concert halls and on the then new phenomenon of the radio. Young pianists were brought up on the Sonata, op. 7, and the *Lyric Pieces* not only in Europe but they were staple teaching material in Russia as well. But then after the second world war Grieg's music seemed to lose ground. Public interest

Grieg's funeral in Bergen.

The last photo of Nina Grieg in 1929 with her niece.

measured in books, records and concert programmes appeared to slacken. Records are a particularly good barometer of interest. When Edward Sackville-West and Desmond Shawe-Taylor published their influential Record Guide in 1951, they could write: "Once so greatly admired, Grieg now tends to be underrated – even despised – in the musical world. This is perhaps inevitable, since the mildly romantic quality of his music is thoroughly out of fashion in our chaotic age of hatred and strife... Debussy's gibe resumes in one fiendish phrase the weaknesses of Grieg's style – its tameness, its extremely limited scope, its feeble optimism; it ignores the lyrical precision, the water-colour beauty of tone and atmosphere he so often achieved."

Of course, his influence in his native country persisted well into the century, and was not just confined to composers of the next generation, like Halvorsen and Sinding whom he knew. Grieg and Norwegian folk song were an inspiration for figures like Ludvig Irgens Jensen and Geirr Tveitt. Of course, there were composers who paid him the compliment of reacting against him – Fartein Valen, whose music enjoyed a brief vogue in both Norway and the English-speaking world in the early 1950s, and whose music abandoned major-minor tonality. Another – and perhaps the most important – is Harald Sæverud who was the first composer to write an entirely modern and brilliant score for *Peer Gynt* immediately after the Second World War. But it is to Grieg and Grieg alone that the wider musical public outside Norway has remained faithful. Even when his

153

music faded from the repertoire in the concert hall, radio or on records, the neglect was relative. It maintained a presence even if it enjoyed less prominence.

For a long time his piano music was relatively neglected in the LP era, roughly speaking from the 1950s through to the mid-1980s. Even the Piano Concerto, once a warhorse that was played almost every day of the week, became almost a rarity. On the BBC's domestic and world services it was heard only four times in 1969 and there was the same tally in 1976 – as many times as Roussel's Third Symphony. The Brahms Violin Concerto by comparison was heard over a dozen times, and the two piano concertos were equally prominent in the BBC's programmes. Less popular Grieg, such as *Haugtussa* or the Cello Sonata was scarcely represented until the 1980s brought about a Grieg renaissance. It was in the 1980s that the Complete Edition of his Works published by Peters of Leipzig, got under way. The complete piano music, as opposed to the ten sets of *Lyric Pieces*, was recorded though not, strangely enough, all the songs, which some would say are the essential Grieg. While every other major song composer from Schubert to Fauré was represented in the CD catalogues, a complete recording of the Grieg songs had to wait until early 1993.

In the year of his death Grieg gave an interview to Arthur Abell, in which he made a prophecy that was as wide of the mark as his future mother-in-law's verdict on him in the 1860s ("He is nothing and he has nothing and he writes music that nobody wants to listen to!"). Perhaps he was indulging in a little false modesty when talking about his achievement he said, "My music will undoubtedly be forgotten in a hundred years' time, nevertheless, I do not feel I have wasted my time, as I have produced music that has given pleasure to millions of people in all enlightened countries... I do not claim to be in the same class as Bach, Mozart and Beethoven. Their works will last for ever, whereas I have written for my own era and my own generation." His music has given pleasure far beyond his time and he would have been surprised at the extent of the celebrations on the 150th anniversary of his birth, in 1993. Grieg Societies have been formed in Norway, Britain, the United States, Germany and Russia. Far from being forgotten, he was celebrated on the most ambitious and extensive scale far beyond the shores of his beloved homeland but throughout the world.

Catalogue of Works

Compositions with Opus numbers

1. Four Piano Pieces. 1861.
2. Four Songs for alto voice and piano. 1861.
3. Six Poetic Tone Pictures for piano. 1863
4. Six Songs for alto voice and piano. 1863-64.
5. Melodies of the Heart (Hans Christian Andersen) for voice and piano. 1864-65.
6. Humoresques for piano. 1865.
7. Piano Sonata in E Minor. 1865
8. Violin Sonata No. 1 in F major. 1865.
9. Songs and Ballads (Andreas Munch) for voice and piano. 1863-66.
1O. Four Songs (Christian Winther) for voice and piano. 1866.
11. *In Autumn.* (Fantasy for piano four hands) 1866. rev Concert Overture *In Autumn* 1887.
12. *Lyric Pieces* for piano.- Book I. 1864(?)-67.
13. Violin Sonata No. 2 in G major. 1867.
14. Two Symphonic Pieces (arrangement for piano four hands of 2nd and 3rd movements of the *Symphony in C minor* (1864). 1869
15. Four Songs for voice and piano 1864-68
16. Piano Concerto in A minor. 1868
17. Twenty-five Norwegian Folk Songs and Dances. 1869.
18. Nine Songs for mezzo sop/bar and piano 1865-69.
19. Pictures from Folk Life. 1869-71.
20. Before a southern convent. 1871 rev 1890
21. Four Songs (Bjørnson) for voice and piano. 1870-72)
22. Sigurd Jorsalfar. Incidental music for Bjørnson's play. 1872.
23. Peer Gynt. Incidental music for Ibsen's play. 1874-75 rev 1885, 1887-88, 1890-92, 1901-02.
24. Ballade in G minor for piano. 1875-76.
25. Six Songs (Ibsen) for voice and piano. 1876.
26. Five Songs (John Poulsen) for voice and piano. 1876.
27. String Quartet in G minor. 1877-78.
28. Album Leaves for piano. 1864-78.
29. Improvisations on Two Norwegian Folk Songs for piano. 1878.
30. Album for male voices. 1877-78.
31. Land Sighting (Landkjenning); for baritone, male chorus and harmonium/organ. 1872. for baritone, male chorus and orch. 1881.
32. The Mountain Thrall (Bergtekne) for baritone, strings and two horns. 1877-78.
33. Twelve Songs (Vinje) cor voice and piano. 1873-80.
34. Two Elegiac Melodies for string orchestra (arrangements of Op. 33, Nos. 2 & 3). 1880.
35. Norwegian Dances for piano four hands. 1880
36. Cello Sonata in A minor. 1881.
37. Waltz Caprices for piano four hands. 1883.
38. *Lyric Pieces* for piano.- Book II. 1883.
39. Six Songs for voice and piano. 1869-84.
40. Holberg Suite. for piano 1884; for string orchestra 1885.
41. Transcription of original songs for piano - I. 1884.
42. Bergliot - melodrama with orchestra, 1871 rev. 1885.
43 *Lyric Pieces* for piano.- Book III. 1886.
44. Reminiscences from Mountain and Fjord (Holger Drachmann) for voice and piano. 1886.
45. Violin Sonata No. 3 in C minor. 1880-87.
46. Peer Gynt Suite No. 1. 1887-88.
47. *Lyric Pieces* for piano.- Book IV. 1885-88
48. Six Songs for voice and piano. 1884 and 1888.
49. Six Songs (Holger Drachmann) for voice and piano. 1886 and 1889.
50. Scenes from *Olav Trygvason* (Bjørjson) for soloists, mixed chorus and orchestra. 1873 rev 1888.
51. Old Norwegian Melody with variations for two pianos 1890; for orchestra 1900-05.
52. Transcription of original songs for piano - II. 1890.
53. Two Melodies for string orchestra. 1890
54. *Lyric Pieces* for piano.- Book V. 1891; Nos 1-4, 6 for orchestra as *Lyric Suite*. 1905.
55. Peer Gynt Suite No. 2. 1890-92.
56. Three Orchestral Pieces from Sigurd Jorsalfar. 1892.
57. *Lyric Pieces* for piano.- Book VI. 1893.
58. Five Songs (John Paulsen) for voice and piano. 1893-94.
59. Six Elegiac Songs (John Paulsen) for voice and piano. 1893-94.
60. Five Songs (Wilhelm Krag) for voice and piano. 1893-94.
61. Seven Children's Songs for voice and piano. 1894.
62. *Lyric Pieces* for piano.- Book VII. 1895.
63. Two Nordic Melodies for string orchestra. 1895.
64. Symphonic Dances; for piano four hands. 1896-97; for orchestra. 1896-98.
65. *Lyric Pieces* for piano.- Book VIII. 1896.
66. Nineteen Norwegian Folk Songs for piano. 1896.
67. Haugtussa (The Mountain Maid) (Arne Garborg) for voice and piano. 1895-98.
68. *Lyric Pieces* for piano.- Book IX. 1898-99.
69. Five Songs (Otto Benzon) for voice and piano. 1900
70. Five Songs (Otto Benzon) for voice and piano. 1900
71. *Lyric Pieces* for piano.- Book X. 1901.
72. Slåtter (Norwegian Peasant Dances) for piano. 1902-03.
73. Stimmung (Moods). 1901-05.
74. Four Psalms for solo baritone and mixed chorus a cappella. 1906.

Compositions without Opus numbers (CW)

CW100. Posthumous Songs for voice and piano.
1865-67.

CW101. Posthumous Songs for voice and piano.
1873-1905.

CW102. Larvik's Polka for piano. 1858.

CW103. Three Pieces for piano. 1858.

CW104. Nine Children's Pieces for piano. 1859

CW105. Short Pieces for piano. 1858-59.

CW106. Look to the Sea, for voice and piano. 1859.

CW107. Three Pieces for piano. 1860.

CW108. The Singing Congregation for alto voice
and piano. 1860.

CW109. Fugue in F minor for string quartet 1861.

CW110. Dona nobis pacem. Fugue for mixed chorus
a cappella.

CW111. Four Songs for male chorus a cappella. 1862.

CW112. Symphony in C minor. 1863-64.

CW116. Agitato for piano. 1865.

CW117. Funeral March for Rikard Nordraak;
for piano 1866;
for wind and percussion 1867 rev 1899.

CW118 Intermezzo in A minor for cello and piano.

CW126. The Princess (Bjørnson) for voice and piano.

CW137. Andante con moto for piano trio. 1878.

CW146. String Quartet No. 2 in F major. 1891.

CW148. Six Songs for voice and orchestra.

CW149. Five Songs (Garborg)
not included in Haugtussa, Op. 67.

Collected Editions

Grieg, Edvard. *Complete Works, Vol.*I-20
(C. F. Peters, Frankfurt/London/New York).

I. INSTRUMENTAL MUSIC

Solo Piano:

1 **Lyric Pieces I-X**

2 **Other Original Compositions**

3 **Arrangements of Norwegian Folk Music**

4 **Arrangements of Own Works**
(ed. Dag Schjelderup-Ebbe)

Piano Four Hands:

5 **Original Compositions and Arrangements
of Own Works** (ed. Rune Andersen)

6 **Dramatic Music** (ed. Nils Grinde) *Two Pianos:*

7 **Original Compositions and Arrangements**
(ed. Arvid Vollsnes)

ChamberMusic:

8 **Sonatas for Violin and Piano, Sonata for Cello
and Piano** (ed. Finn Benestad)

9 **String Quartets, Other Chamber Music,
Arrangements of Own Works for
Chamber Orchestra** (ed. Finn Benestad)

Orchestra:

10. **Piano Concerto in A Minor** (ed. Kjell Skyllstad)
n. Original Compositions (ed. Finn Benestad
and Gunnar Rugstad)
Suites for Orchestra (ed. Finn Benestad
and Dag Schjelderup-Ebbe)
Arrangements of Own Works and Compositions
without Opus Numbers (ed. Gunnar Rugstad)

II. VOCAL MUSIC

Songs with Piano Accompaniment:
Songs Op. 2-49 (ed. Dan Fog and Nils Grinde)
Songs Op. 58-70 and songs without Opus Numbers
(ed. Dan Fog and Nils Grinde)
Vocal Compositions with Orchestra:
6. Original Compositions and Arrangements of Own Works
(ed. Hans Magne Graesvold)
Unaccompanied Choral Music:
Original Compositions and Arrangements of Own Works
(ed. Dan Fog)

III. DRAMATIC MUSIC

8. Peer Gynt (ed. Finn Benestad)
Other Original Compositions (ed. Finn Benestad)

IV. APPENDIX

20. Addenda and Corrigenda (ed. Finn Benestad
and Dag Schjelderup-Ebbe)

Select Bibliography

Books

Abraham, Gerald (ed.)
Edvard Grieg. A Symposium. London, 1948.
Bailie, Eleanor.
Grieg. The Pianist's Repertoire. London, 1993.
Benestad, Finn & Schelderup-Ebbe, Dag.
Edvard Grieg.The Man and the Artist.
(tr. William H. Halverson and Leland B. Sateren)
Edvard Grieg: Chamber Music: Nationalism, Universality,
Individuality.
Oslo, 1993.
Carley, Lionel.
Grieg and Delius. A Chronicle of their Friendship
in Letters. London, 1994.
Finck, Henry T.
Edvard Grieg. New York, 1906.(New and enlarged
edition, New York, 1909.)
Grieg and his Music. New York, 1929.
Fischer, Kurt von.
Griegs Harmonik und die nordlandische Folklore.
Bern and Leipzig, 1938.
Fog, Dan.
Grieg-Katalog (in Danish and German).
Copenhagen, 1980.
Foss, Hubert.
Edvard Hagerup Grieg. *The Heritage of Music.*
Oxford, 1951.
Foster, Beryl.
The Songs of Edvard Grieg. Aldershot, 1990.
Grieg, Edvard.
Dagbøker (Diaries) ed. Finn Benestad.
Bergen, 1993.
Horton, John.
Grieg. (The Master Musicians Series). London, 1974.
Monrad Johansen, David.
Edvard Grieg. Oslo, 1934
(English trans. by Madge Robertson.) Princeton, 1938.
Schjelderup-Ebbe, Dag.
A Study of Grieg's Harmony: With Special Reference to his
Contributions to Musical Impressionism. Oslo, 1953.
Edvard Grieg. 1858-67 (with special reference to the
evolution of his harmonic style). London, 1964.
Schlotel, Brian. *Grieg.* BBC Music Guides, London, 1986.

Articles

Carley, Lionel.
Grieg and Musical Life in England. Musik
& forskning 1993-94, Copenhagen, 1994.
Dale, Kathleen.
"Edvard Grieg's Pianoforte Music."
Music and Letters, 1943.
"Grieg Discoveries." *Monthly Musical Record,* 1954.
Desmond, Astra.
"Grieg's Songs." *Music and Letters,* 1943.
Grainger, Percy Aldridge.
"Personal Recollections of Grieg." *Musical Times,* 1907.
"Personal Recollections of Edvard Grieg."
The Etude, 1943.
"Grieg's Last Opus." *Hinrichsen's Musical Year Book,*
London, 1952.
Grieg, J. Russell.
"Grieg and his Scottish Ancestry."
Hinrichsen's Musical Year Book, London, 1952.
Horton, John.
"Grieg's Slåtter for piano". *Music and Letters,*
London, 1945.
"Ibsen, Grieg and Peer Gynt", *Music and Letters,*
London, 1945.

General

Abraham, Gerald.
A Hundred Years of Music. (4th ed)
London, 1974.
The Concise Oxford History of Music. Oxford, 1980.
Grinde, Nils.
Norsk musikkhistorie. Olso. 1971.
Haugen, Einar & Cai, Camilla.
Ole Bull: Norway's Romantic Musician and
Cosmopolitan Patriot. Madison, 1993.
Horton, John.
Scandinavian Music. A Short History.
London, 1963.
Lange, Kristian.
Norwegian Music, A Survey. Oslo, 1971.
Støverud, Torbjørn.
Milestones of Norwegian Literature.
Oslo, 1971.

Index

*Illustrations are indicated in **bold** type*